Using Picture Books to Teach Language Arts Standards in Grades 3–5

Using Picture Books to Teach Language Arts Standards in Grades 3–5

Written and Illustrated by
Brenda S. Copeland and Patricia A. Messner

LIBRARIES
U N L I M I T E D
A Member of the Greenwood Publishing Group

Westport, Connecticut • London

Library of Congress Cataloging-in-Publication Data

Copeland, Brenda S.
  Using picture books to teach language arts standards in grades 3–5 / written and illustrated by Brenda S. Copeland and Patricia A. Messner.
      p. cm.
  Includes bibliographical references and index.
  ISBN 1-59158-319-5 (pbk. : alk. paper)
  1. Picture books for children—Educational aspects—United States. 2. Language arts—Standards—United States.
I. Messner, Patricia A. II. Title.
LB1044.9.P49C665   2006
372.133'5—dc22   2006003714

British Library Cataloguing in Publication Data is available.

Library of Congress Catalog Card Number: 2006003714
ISBN: 1-59158-319-5

First published in 2006

Libraries Unlimited, 88 Post Road West, Westport, CT 06881
A Member of the Greenwood Publishing Group, Inc.
www.lu.com

Printed in the United States of America

The paper used in this book complies with the
Permanent Paper Standard issued by the National
Information Standards Organization (Z39.48-1984).

10 9 8 7 6 5 4 3 2 1

Dedicated to the extraordinary third-, fourth-, and fifth-grade students at Donovan, Northside, and Pine Street Elementary Schools. Thanks for all your help.

Contents

Preface. ix

National Language Arts Standards. xi

Part One:
Sequencing the Plot Favorites

Third Grade

Chocolatina 3

The Memory String. 5

Silver Packages 9

Fourth Grade

Bad Boys. 12

The Bunyans. 15

More Than Anything Else. 18

The Remarkable Farkle McBride. 21

Sody Sallyratus. 23

When Jessie Came Across the Sea 26

Fifth Grade

Testing Miss Malarkey. 32

Part Two:
Comprehension Favorites

Third Grade

Aunt Flossie's Hats and Crab Cakes Later 37

Look Out, Jack! The Giant Is Back!. 40

The Seven Silly Eaters 43

Fourth Grade

The Blizzard 46

The Lady in the Box 51

The Purple Coat. 54

Shoeless Joe & Black Betty 58

Fifth Grade

Pink and Say. 61

The Rag Coat 67

Sister Anne's Hands 70

Part Three:
Story Elements Favorites

Third Grade

Muncha! Muncha! Muncha! 75

Tacky and the Emperor 80

Fourth Grade

Bigfoot Cinderrrrrella 82

The Christmas Miracle of Jonathan Toomey 85

Gullywasher Gulch 88

Petite Rouge: A Cajun Red Riding Hood 91

The Seven Chinese Sisters 95

Rumpelstiltskin's Daughter 98

Fifth Grade

The Magic Nesting Doll 100

Souperchicken 103

Part Four:
Biography Favorites

Third Grade

Abe Lincoln Remembers 109

Brave Harriet 112

Hank Aaron: Brave in Every Way 116

Martin's Big Words 120

Fourth Grade

Abbie Against the Storm 124

The Heroine of the Titanic 127

My Great-Aunt Arizona 130

Thomas Jefferson: A Picture Book Biography 133

Fifth Grade

Betty Doll 136

Hiding from the Nazis 139

Appendix 143

Bibliography 147

Web Resources 153

Index 155

Preface

Since the publication of our first book, *Linking Picture Books to Standards*, colleagues and friends have encouraged us to write a book of lesson plans using picture books for the third, fourth, and fifth grades. When we accepted this challenge, we rediscovered some great picture books that were getting lost on the shelfs because the reading level was higher than the usual readers of picture books. We hope our lessons motivate teachers and school librarians to incorporate some of these awesome stories and authors into their upper elementary curriculum. Our challenge to our readers is that these books be used to introduce units and studies that are already established in upper grade level classes. Many of these stories will create additional writing opportunities and encourage students to read more.

Our lessons have been tested in our library classrooms and are aligned with the national language arts standards from the National Council of Teachers of English. They can be found at www.ncte.org and also in *Standards for the English Language Arts* (sponsored by National Council of Teachers of English and International Reading Association; Urbana, IL: NCTE, 1996). Questions for the comprehension section of this book have been designed using *Benjamin Bloom's Taxonomy of Educational Objectives: Handbook I, The Cognitive Domain* (New York: David McKay, 1956). We designed these lessons for forty-five minutes of library or classroom time. Many lessons can become part of units that third, fourth, and fifth graders cover in the classroom curriculum.

There are four sections in this book: Sequencing the Plot, Comprehension, Story Elements, and Biographies. Each lesson lists the applicable language arts national standards and provides objectives, skills, and worksheets, together with a list of the materials needed. At the end of many of the lessons, we have listed other titles from this same genre or author that can be used for extra writing projects and research options. We have found that teachers like to have a list in hand from which to choose books for classroom reading centers and writing stations. We hope they will become an added bonus to this collection of lesson plans.

*National Language Arts Standards**

NL-ENG.K-12.1 Reading for Perspective

Students read a wide range of print and nonprint texts to build an understanding of texts, of themselves, and of the cultures of the United States and the world; to acquire new information; to respond to the needs and demands of society and the workplace; and for personal fulfillment. Among these texts are fiction and nonfiction, classic and contemporary works

NL-ENG.K-12.2 Understanding the Human Experience

Students read a wide range of literature from many periods in many genres to build an understanding of many dimensions (e.g., philosophical, ethical, aesthetic) of human experience.

NL-ENG.K-12.3 Evaluation Strategies

Students apply a wide range of strategies to comprehend, interpret, evaluate, and appreciate texts. They draw on their prior experience, their interactions with other readers and writers, their knowledge of word meaning and of other texts, their word identification strategies, and their understanding of textual features (e.g., sound-letter correspondence, sentence structure, context, graphics).

NL-ENG.K-12.4 Communication Skills

Students adjust their use of spoken, written, and visual language (e.g., conventions, style, vocabulary) to communicate effectively with a variety of audiences and for different purposes.

NL-ENG.K-12.5 Communication Strategies

Students employ a wide range of strategies as they write and use different writing process elements appropriately to communicate with different audiences for a variety of purposes.

NL-ENG.K-12.6 Applying Knowledge

Students apply knowledge of language structure, language conventions (e.g., spelling and punctuation), media techniques, figurative language, and genre to create, critique, and discuss print and nonprint texts.

NL-ENG.K-12.7 Evaluating Data

Students conduct research on issues and interest by generating ideas and questions, and by posing problems. They gather, evaluate, and synthesize data from a variety of sources (e.g., print and nonprint texts, artifacts, people) to communicate their discoveries in ways that suit their purpose and audience.

NL-ENG.K-12.8 Developing Research Skills

Students use a variety of technological and informational resources (e.g., libraries, databases, computer networks, video) to gather and synthesize information and to create and communicate knowledge.

NL-ENG.K-12.9 Multicultural Understanding

Students develop an understanding of and respect for diversity in language use, patterns, and dialects across cultures, ethic groups, geographic regions, and social roles.

NL-ENG.K-12.11 Participating in Society

Students participate as knowledgeable, reflective, creative, and critical members of a variety of literacy communities.

NL-ENG.K-12.12 Applying Language Skills

Students use spoken, written, and visual language to accomplish their own purposes (e.g., for learning, enjoyment, persuasion, and the exchange of information).

Standards for the English Language Arts, by the International Reading Association and the National Council of Teachers of English, Copyright 1996 by the International Reading Association and the National Council of Teachers of English. Reprinted with permission.

Part One

Sequencing the Plot Favorites

Chocolatina

by Erik Kraft

Kraft, Erik. *Chocolatina.* New York: Scholastic, 2004.

Objective: Students will listen to the story, write the main events in the story, and arrange the events in order.

Language Arts National Standards

NL-ENG.K-12.4 Communication Skills

Students adjust their use of spoken, written, and visual language (e.g., conventions, style, vocabulary) to communicate effectively with a variety of audiences and for different purposes.

NL-ENG.K-12.5 Communication Strategies

Students employ a wide range of strategies as they write and use different writing process elements appropriately to communicate with different audiences for a variety of purposes.

Skills

- Sequencing the plot

Grade Level: Third grade

Materials

- Water-based markers
- Pattern for candy-bar wrapper copied for each group

Preparing Materials: Copy three or four candy-bar wrappers for each group. Cut out before lesson.

Step 1: Introduce author and title. Tell students to enjoy the story and remind them that they will need to remember the main events in the story.

Step 2: Read the story and allow for comments. This story is very funny, and the students will likely have many comments.

Step 3: Divide the class into three groups. Give each group markers and three or four candy-bar wrappers. Assign each group part of the story. Examples: Group 1—beginning of the story to the part where Chocolatina wishes she was what she eats. Group 2—Chocolatina is asleep until the beginning of health class. Group 3—health class until the end of the story.

Step 4: Tell students to write the main events from their part of the story on the candy-bar wrappers.

Step 5: Gather the class together and arrange the main events in order.

The Memory String

by Eve Bunting

Bunting, Eve. *The Memory String*. New York: Clarion Books, 2000.

Objective: Students will retell the story using a shoestring and buttons.

Language Arts National Standards

NL-ENG.K-12.4 Communication Skills

Students adjust their use of spoken, written, and visual language (e.g., conventions, style, vocabulary) to communicate effectively with a variety of audiences and for different purposes.

NL-ENG.K-12.5 Communication Strategies

Students employ a wide range of strategies as they write and use different writing process elements appropriately to communicate with different audiences for a variety of purposes.

Skills

- Retelling
- Sequencing

Grade Level: Third and fourth grades

Materials

- Long shoestring
- Copy button pattern onto card stock
- Copy worksheet for each student

Preparing materials: Write events on the buttons. Color, cut out, and laminate the buttons. Punch holes in the buttons. Complete the worksheet before beginning the lesson.

Step 1: Introduce the book *The Memory String* by Eve Bunting.

Step 2: Read the book and discuss characters, setting, the problem, and the solution.

Step 3: Retell the story using the shoestring and buttons.

Step 4: Have two students hold the ends of the shoestring as you retell the story. Pass out the buttons to the remaining students.

Step 5: Have other students string buttons on the shoestring as the events are retold. Two students at a time will string a button on the shoestring. Correct as needed.

Step 6: Share a completed worksheet, having filled it out ahead of time with events from your life.

Step 7: Students begin the worksheet by writing their birthday on the first line. They also write a statement on the last line about their current classroom. (Example: "I am in Mrs. Jones's third-grade class at Donovan Elementary.") Tell the students to fill in the other lines with events from their lives. (Example: "I received a red bike for my sixth birthday.")

Teacher's Notes:

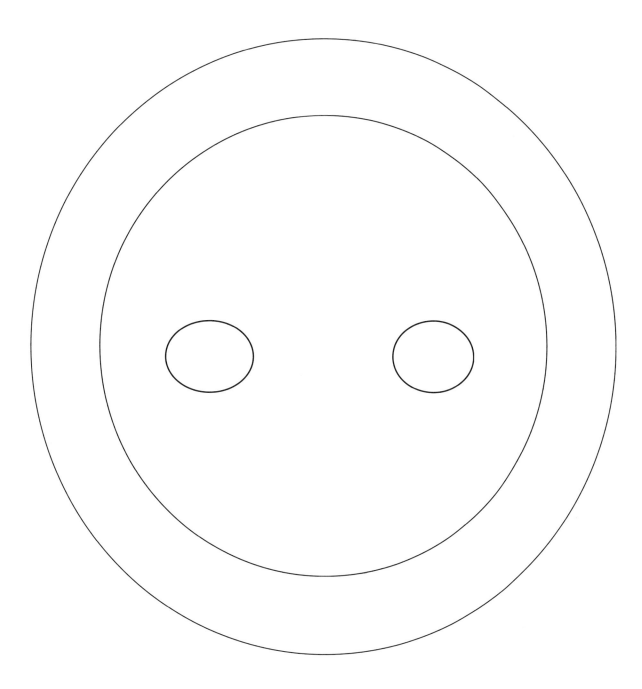

Write your memories on the lines below.
My Memory String

By _____

_____

_____

_____

_____

_____

_____

_____

Silver Packages

by Cynthia Rylant

Rylant, Cynthia. *Silver Packages: An Appalachian Christmas Story*. New York: Orchard Books, 1997.

Objective: Students will retell the story correctly in sequence as the silver package is passed around the group.

Language Arts National Standards

NL-ENG.K-12.4 Communication Skills

Students adjust their use of spoken, written, and visual language (e.g., conventions, style, vocabulary) to communicate effectively with a variety of audiences and for different purposes.

NL-ENG.K-12.5 Communication Strategies

Students employ a wide range of strategies as they write and use different writing process elements appropriately to communicate with different audiences for a variety of purposes.

Skills

- Sequencing the plot
- Creative writing

Grade Level: Third and fourth grades

Materials

- Small package wrapped in silver paper

Step 1: Using the author's note in the preface, explain where the idea for this story came from and what part is true. Point out that this is the same author who wrote the Henry and Mudge books.

Step 2: Read the story and share the pictures as you read.

Step 3: Let students retell the story by passing the silver package. Each student holds the package and tells part of the story in the correct order then passes the package to someone else. Stress that students need to focus on the events as they unfolded in the book. Some will want to tell too much, and others will skip to a part that they remember. Keep the storytelling time moving so that all children have time to share.

Step 4: Explain the worksheet and allow time for students to complete it.

Closure: Gather students and share the worksheets.

Reading Resource Books

Houston, Gloria. *The Year of the Perfect Christmas Tree: An Appalachian Story.* New York: Dial Books for Young Readers, 1988.

Lasky, Kathryn. *Christmas After All: The Great Depression Diary of Minnie Swift.* New York: Scholastic, 2001.

Teacher's Notes:

Silver Packages
By Cynthia Rylant

Writing Worksheet

Pretend you are waiting for the Christmas train. What do you want to find in your silver package? Why? Write your answer in the box below and remember to use complete sentences.

Bad Boys

by Margie Palatini

Palatini, Margie. *Bad Boys.* New York: HarperCollins, 2003.

Objective: Students will complete the worksheet on sequencing after hearing the story.

Language Arts National Standards

NL-ENG.K-12.4 Communication Skills

Students adjust their use of spoken, written, and visual language (e.g., conventions, style, vocabulary) to communicate effectively with a variety of audiences and for different purposes.

NL-ENG.K-12.5 Communication Strategies

Students employ a wide range of strategies as they write and use different writing process elements appropriately to communicate with different audiences for a variety of purposes.

Skills

- Sequencing the plot
- Text-to-text connections with other stories and rhymes

Grade Level: Fourth grade

Materials

- Scrap paper and pencils

Step 1: Introduce the book by asking the students to recall stories that they remember in which a wolf plays a major part in the plot. Make a list on the board. Ask students to explain whether the wolf was portrayed as the good guy or the bad guy. Use the books listed at the end of the lesson for recall if necessary.

Step 2: Share the title of this story and explain that the wolves are in trouble again. Because this author uses word phrases and characters that are related to nursery rhymes and other picture books, ask students to listen for these so that the class can make a list at the end of the story (example: Peep Sheep—Little Bo Beep). Students should jot down these words or phrases on the scrap paper as you read.

Step 3: Read the story and share the pictures.

Step 4: Share what the students observed and make a list on the board. List the phrase and then the story or rhyme to which it connects.

Closure: Independent practice on sequencing. Hand out the worksheet and go over the directions.

Reading Resource Books

Ernst, Lisa Campbell. *Little Red Riding Hood: A Newfangled Prairie Tale*. New York: Simon & Schuster Books for Young Readers, 1995.

Laverde, Arlene. *Alaska's Three Pigs*. Seattle: PAWS IV/Sasquatch Books, 2000.

Trivizas, Eugene. *The Three Little Wolves and the Big Bad Pig*. New York: Margaret K. McElderry Books, 1993.

Wiesner, David. *The Three Pigs*. New York: Clarion Books, 2001.

Teacher's Notes:

Sequencing Worksheet

Number the statements in the order they happen in the story.

_____ Willy and Wally Wolf dress up and pretend to be sheep.

_____ Willy and Wally are in trouble and on the run.

_____ The bad boys are knitting long johns until their hair grows back.

_____ The wolves get a buzz cut.

_____ The sheep start noticing that Wally and Willy have big ears, big eyes, and lousy wool coats.

_____ Wally and Willy introduce themselves as the "Peep Sheep."

_____ Betty Mutton suggest that she has a cure for the lousy wool coats.

_____ The bad wolves head for the hills.

Where are Wally and Willy headed next? Write a sequel to this story.

_____

_____

_____

_____

_____

_____

_____

_____

_____

_____

The Bunyans

by Audrey Wood

Wood, Audrey. *The Bunyans.* New York: The Blue Sky Press, 1996.

Objective: Students will listen to the story, research the natural wonders discussed therein, and sequence the travels of Paul Bunyan on a U.S. map.

Language Arts National Standards

NL-ENG.K-12.8 Developing Research Skills

Students use a variety of technological and information resources (e.g., libraries, databases, computer networks, video) to gather and synthesize information and to create and communicate knowledge.

Skills

- Researching
- Sequencing

Grade Level: Fourth grade

Materials

- Large index cards
- Markers
- Map of the United States
- Construction paper
- Pencils and worksheets

Preparing Materials: Write the six natural wonders mentioned in the story each on its own large index cards. Natural wonders: Mammoth Cave, Niagara Falls, Bryce Canyon, Old Faithful, Rocky Mountains, and the Great Sand Dunes. Display a map of the United States on the chalkboard. Cut the numbers 1 through 6 out of construction paper and laminate.

Step 1: Introduce the title, author, and illustrator. Talk about natural wonders. Explain to students that they will need to listen for six natural wonders as you read the story.

Step 2: Read the story and then list the natural wonders on the board that the students recall.

Step 3: Divide class into six groups. Each group will locate and research the natural wonders in atlases and encyclopedias and on the Internet. Allow time for students to complete research.

Step 4: Gather students and share information. Plot the natural wonders on the U.S. map as students share what they have learned. Use numbers to sequence the wonders as they appear in the story.

Web Site Resources

http://www.mammoth.cave.national-park.com/info.htm#mc

http://www.niagarafallslive.com/Facts_about_Niagara_Falls.htm

http://www.npca.org/explore_the_parks/new_parks/greatsanddunes.asp

http://www.nps.gov/yell/tours/oldfaithful/

http://www.desertusa.com/bryce/

http://biology.usgs.gov/s+t/SNT/noframe/wm146.htm

Teacher's Notes:

Worksheet

Names of students in your group _____

_____

Name of natural wonder _____

Locate your natural wonder in the atlas using the most efficient process. Describe the process of locating your wonder. _____

_____

_____

_____

_____

_____

Find and describe the size of your natural wonder. Examples: height, length, total number of acres, amount of water.

_____

_____

In what state is your natural wonder located? _____

List three special features about your natural wonder.

     1. _____

     2. _____

     3. _____

In what order was your natural wonder mentioned in the story?

_____

_____

_____

More Than Anything Else

by Marie Bradby

Bradby, Marie. *More Than Anything Else.* New York: Orchard Books, 1995.

Objective: Students will sequence the plot and complete the worksheet.

Language Arts National Standards

NL-ENG.K-12.4 Communication Skills

Students adjust their use of spoken, written, and visual language (e.g., conventions, style, vocabulary) to communicate effectively with a variety of audiences and for different purposes.

NL-ENG.K-12.5 Communication Strategies

Students employ a wide range of strategies as they write and use different writing process elements appropriately to communicate with different audiences for a variety of purposes.

Skills

- Sequencing the plot
- Creative writing

Grade Level: Fourth grade

Materials

- Worksheet for each student
- Full sheet from a newspaper
- Magic marker (heavy enough tip to write over newsprint)
- Easel
- An old-looking lantern and book
- An old hat and a man's vest

Preparing Materials: Attach the newspaper to the easel with tape and set aside for easy access after you have finished reading the story.

Step 1: Dress in the old hat and vest. Greet the students with the lantern and book in hand.

Step 2: Introduce the lesson by telling the students that you have something to share that is special and that you wanted it "more than anything else" in the world.

Step 3: Tell the story in character.

Step 4: Since the man reading the newspaper in the story plays an important part in this narrative, use the newspaper and easel you have prepared ahead of time to record a list of important

18

steps in the story using a dark magic marker. Record these as the students recall the plot of the book.

Closure: Hand out the worksheet and go over the directions. Students can complete them independently.

Reading Resource Books

Bogart, Jo Ellen. *Jeremiah Learns to Read.* New York: Orchard Books, 1997.

DeClements, Barthe. *6th Grade Can Really Kill You.* New York: Viking Kestrel, 1985.

Giff, Patricia Reilly. *The Beast in Ms. Rooney's Room.* New York: Dell, 1984.

Polacco, Patricia. *Thank You, Mr. Falker.* New York: Philomel Books, 1998.

Williams, Suzanne. *Library Lil.* New York: Dial Books for Young Readers, 1997.

Teacher's Notes:

Booker T. Washington

Think about the effect the newspaperman had on Booker T. Washington. Explain the steps that Booker followed after he saw the man and how he made Booker's dream of learning to read come true.

Step 1.	

What would you like to learn to do? Complete the following statement and give reasons for your answer.

Like Booker, I want to do something more than anything else in the whole wide world. I want to learn how to _____

_____

_____

_____

_____

The Remarkable Farkle McBride

by John Lithgow

Lithgow, John. *The Remarkable Farkle McBride.* New York: Simon & Schuster Books for Young Readers, 2000.

Objective: Students will correctly sequence Farkle's musical history and arrange it the instruments in order of their difficulty to play. After the sequencing, students should be able to justify their opinion.

Language Arts National Standards

NL-ENG.K-12.4 Communication Skills

Students adjust their use of spoken, written, and visual language (e.g., conventions, style, vocabulary) to communicate effectively with a variety of audiences and for different purposes.

NL-ENG.K-12.5 Communication Strategies

Students employ a wide range of strategies as they write and use different writing process elements appropriately to communicate with different audiences for a variety of purposes.

Skills

- Sequencing
- Comprehension

Grade Level: Fourth grade

Materials

- Worksheets and pencils for each student

Step 1: Introduce the title and author. Show students the author picture and read the biography. Talk about John Lithgow as an author together with his other accomplishments.

Step 2: Tell students to be ready to recall the musical instruments in the story after reading it.

Step 3: Read the story and allow for comments.

Step 4: With the students' help, write the names of the musical instruments that appear in the story on the board.

Step 5: Explain the worksheet. Students arrange the names of the instruments in the order they appear in the story on the first musical staff. According to their opinions, the students arrange the instruments in order from easiest to hardest in terms of how difficult they are to learn how to play. Students justify their choices. Allow time for students to complete worksheets.

Step 6: Gather students back together and share worksheets to discuss and compare and contrast their answers.

Sequence the plot on the musical staff below.

List below the instruments Farkle played from easiest to hardest to play and explain your answers.

_____

_____

_____

Sody Sallyratus

Retold and illustrated by Teri Sloat

Sloat, Teri. *Sody Sallyratus*. New York: Dutton Children's Books, 1997.

Objective: Students will sequence the plot and complete the worksheet.

Language Arts National Standards

NL-ENG.K-12.1 Reading for Perspective

Students read a wide range of print and nonprint texts to build an understanding of texts, of themselves, and of the cultures of the United States and the world; to acquire new information; to respond to the needs and demands of society and the workplace; and for personal fulfillment. Among these texts are fiction and nonfiction, classic and contemporary works.

NL-ENG.K-12.2 Understanding the Human Experience

Students read a wide range of literature from many periods in many genres to build an understanding of many dimensions (e.g., philosophical, ethical, aesthetic) of human experience.

NL-ENG.K-12.3 Evaluation Strategies

Students apply a wide range of strategies to comprehend, interpret, evaluate, and appreciate texts. They draw on their prior experience, their interactions with other readers and writers, their knowledge of word meaning and of other texts, their word identification strategies, and their understanding of textual features (e.g., sound-letter correspondence, sentence structure, context, graphics).

NL-ENG.K-12.9 Multicultural Understanding

Students develop an understanding of and respect for diversity in language use, patterns, and dialects across cultures, ethic groups, geographic regions, and social roles.

Skills

- Sequencing the plot

Grade Level: Fourth grade

Materials

- Atlas showing the Appalachian Mountains (*Doubleday Children's Atlas* or others)
- Overhead page listing of characters
- *Kane's Famous First Facts*
- *World Book Encyclopedia* or others
- Seven index cards
- Rolling pin and mixing bowl
- Large bibbed apron

Preparing Materials: Write the following words, one each on index cards: old woman, old man, little girl, little boy, squirrel, Appalachian Mountains, and baking soda

Step 1: Explain to the students that this story comes from the Appalachian Mountain region of the United States. Some of the words and expressions might seem different from what they are accustomed to hearing.

Step 2: Ask students to listen for the words "Sody Sody Sody Sallyratus." Sing-song this phrase each time you use it and ask the students to join in on the fun. Kids of all ages love this story and will like to take part in the telling of this tale.

Step 3: Dress in the apron and tell the story. Use the mixing bowl and rolling pin as props as you move through the narration. Remind the students to help with the Sody Sallyratus phrase.

Step 4: After the story, ask students whether they can determine what the sody is in the story. What is the modern word we use for it today? Share the last page that explains what baking soda can be used for. (You might wish to save this page until the end if you have one of the groups research baking soda.)

Step 5: Divide the class into seven groups and give out the cards that you have prepared ahead of time. Explain that the groups with the characters written on their index cards will discuss what happened when that character went to the store for the Sody Sallyratus. They will write out two sentences that explain the events that occurred during that part of the story and will be prepared to report back to the group. The other two groups will either look up the Appalachian Mountains in the atlas or research information on baking soda. They will also write two sentences on what they discovered and be prepared to report back to the group.

Closure: Students will return to the group and share sentences. Write character sentences on the overhead. This provides a sequencing of the major events in the story. The last two groups report on the information and bring the lesson to a conclusion.

Reading Resource Books

Hiser, Berniece T. *The Adventure of Charlie and His Wheat-Straw Hat: A Memorat.* New York: Dodd, Mead, 1986.

Isaacs, Anne. *Swamp Angel.* New York: Dutton Children's Books, 1994.

Nolen, Jerdine. *Thunder Rose.* Orlando, FL: Silver Whistle/Harcourt, 2003.

Teacher's Notes:

Baking Soda

Little boy

Little girl

Old man

Old woman

Squirrel

When Jessie Came Across the Sea

by Amy Hest

Hest, Amy. *When Jessie Came Across the Sea.* Cambridge, MA: Candlewick Press, 1997.

Objective: Students will recall the main part of the story and complete the suitcase worksheet.

Language Arts National Standards

NL-ENG.K-12.4 Communication Skills

Students adjust their use of spoken, written, and visual language (e.g., conventions, style, vocabulary) to communicate effectively with a variety of audiences and for different purposes.

NL-ENG.K-12.5 Communication Strategies

Students employ a wide range of strategies as they write and use different writing process elements appropriately to communicate with different audiences for a variety of purposes.

Skills

- Sequencing the plot
- Creative writing

Grade Level: Fourth grade

Materials

- Pieces of lace or a handkerchief
- Needle and thread
- Satchel or old suitcase
- Jar with coins inside
- Overhead transparency made from the jar pattern
- Scarf to tie around head

Step 1: Open the suitcase and display the props that have been collected. Tie the scarf around your head and explain that all of these items play an important part in the plot of the story.

Step 2: Read the story and share the pictures.

Step 3: Using the overhead of the jar, lead the students in a discussion of the story. Ask students how Jessie used the jar. Make a list on the jar of the events that occurred after Jessie arrived in the United States.

Step 4: Estimate how long Jessie would have worked for her grandmother's passage. Use the picture clues and text to help answer this question. Review text if students need prompting.

Step 5: Read directions for the "Pack Your Suitcase" worksheet and give students time to work independently.

Closure: Set aside time to share and to read aloud what students have packed inside their suitcases.

Optional Research Activity

Objective: Students will visit the Ellis Island Web site and complete the research worksheet.

Language Arts National Standards

NL-ENG.K-12.8 Developing Research Skills

Students use a variety of technological and informational resources (e.g., libraries, databases, computer networks, video) to gather and synthesize information and to create and communicate knowledge.

Skills

- Navigating a Web site
- Researching

Materials

- A collection of encyclopedias and other nonfiction books about Ellis Island and immigration to the United States at the time of the story
- A worksheet for each group

Step 1: Divide the class into small groups depending on the number of computers in your library/media center setup. Pass out worksheets and rotate the students so that each group has computer time. As groups finish working on the computers, the other resources will provide additional resources for them to read and research. Additional facts can be listed on the bottom of the worksheet. If you have limited computers, this will keep students on task while they wait for their turns.

Step 2: Guide the students through the following steps to visit the Ellis Island Web site:

    a. Type in the URL (Web site address)—www.ellisisland.com.

    b. Click on "Immigration in the United States."

    c. Click on "Interactive Tour of Ellis Island from Scholastic."

    d. Follow the directions on the worksheet and answer the questions.

Reading Resource Books

Bunting, Eve. *Dreaming of America: An Ellis Island Story*. New York: Bridge Water Books, 2000.

Jacobs, William. *Ellis Island: New Hope in a New Land*. New York: C. Scribner's, 1990.

Levine, Ellen. *If Your Name Was Changed at Ellis Island*. New York: Scholastic, 1993.

Woodruff, Elvira. *The Memory Coat*. New York: Scholastic, 1999.

Teacher's Notes:

Pack Your Suitcase Worksheet

Pretend you were coming to America as an immigrant like Jessie in our story. List what you would pack to bring with you in the top half of the suitcase and the reasons you would bring these things in the bottom half.

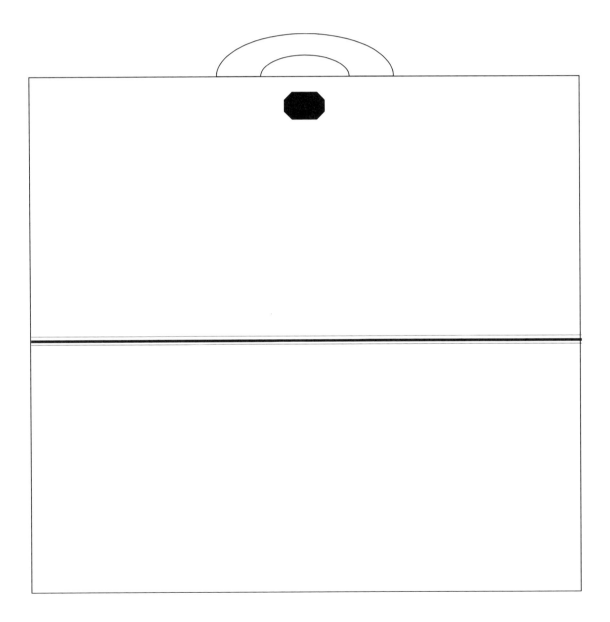

What did Jessie do after she came to America?
List these events in the correct order inside the jar.

In America.....

When Jessie Came Across the Sea
By Amy Hest

Research Worksheet

Type in the URL (address of Web site): **www.ellisisland.com.**
Click on **"Immigration in the United States."**
Click on **"Interactive Tour of Ellis Island from Scholastic."**
Click on **"Start Tour."**
Play through the tour of slides and answer the following questions.

1. How many immigrants passed through the doors of Ellis Island? _____

2. When did Ellis Island open its doors to immigrants? _____

3. Who was the first to arrive at Ellis Island? _____

4. Why were the immigrants given a medical exam? _____

_____

_____

_____

Record some awesome facts that your group uncovered from this research.

_____

_____

_____

_____

_____

_____

_____

_____

From *Using Picture Books to Teach Language Arts Standards in Grades 3–5,* written and illustrated by Brenda S. Copeland and Patricia A. Messner. Westport, CT: Libraries Unlimited. Copyright © 2006.

Testing Miss Malarkey

by Judy Finchler

Finchler, Judy. *Testing Miss Malarkey*. New York: Walker, 2000.

Objective: Students will connect phrases and words to other stories and rhymes and complete the worksheet about sequencing.

Language Arts National Standards

NL-ENG.K-12.1 Reading for Perspective

Students read a wide range of print and nonprint texts to build an understanding of texts, of themselves, and of the cultures of the United States and the world; to acquire new information; to respond to the needs and demands of society and the workplace; and for personal fulfillment. Among these texts are fiction and nonfiction, classic and contemporary works.

NL-ENG.K-12.2 Understanding the Human Experience

Students read a wide range of literature from many periods in many genres to build an understanding of many dimensions (e.g., philosophical, ethical, aesthetic) of human experience.

Skills

- Sequencing the plot
- Creative writing

Grade Level: Fifth grade

Materials

- Worksheet for each student

Step 1: Introduce the book and share the cover. Ask the students to look and listen for the main events in the story.

Step 2: Read the story and share the book.

Step 3: This age group will understand the colorful way the author describes the school and the names that she picks for the teachers and staff. For example, Mrs. Magenta is the art teacher. Spend some time going over things that they observed about the story. Younger students will not understand these, but older children enjoy pointing them out.

Closure: Explain the worksheet and give students time for completion. Go over the worksheet as a class and make a list of events on the board or overhead after individual work time.

Reading Resource Books

Finchler, Judy. *Miss Malarkey Won't Be in Today*. New York: Walker, 1998.
Finchler, Judy. *Miss Malarkey's Field Trip*. New York: Walker, 2004.
Finchler, Judy. *You're a Sport, Miss Malarkey*. New York: Walker, 1998.

1. **Start at number 1 and record the events of the story as you move around the pie.**

2. **On the back of this paper, write a descriptive paragraph about an important test that you took in your classroom. Explain what happened and describe the crazy events about how you survived the test.**

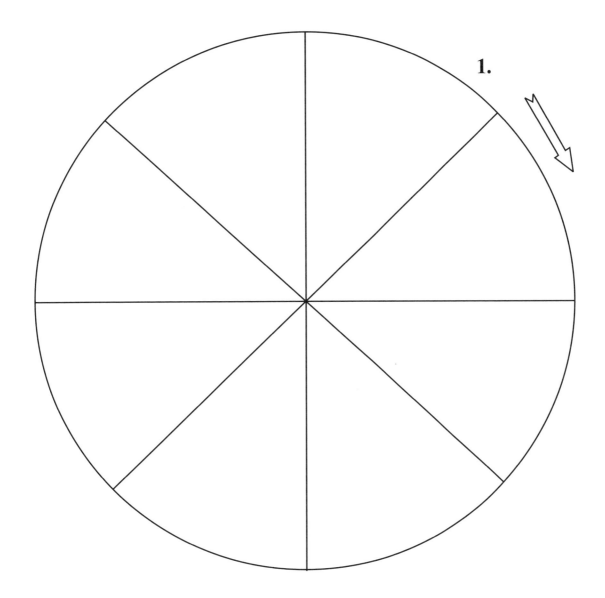

Part Two

Comprehension Favorites

Aunt Flossie's Hats and Crab Cakes Later

by Elizabeth Fitzgerald Howard

Howard, Elizabeth Fitzgerald. *Aunt Flossie's Hats and Crab Cakes Later.* New York: Clarion Books, 2001.

Objective: Students will listen to the story and correctly answer comprehension questions.

Language Arts National Standards

NL-ENG.K-12.3 Evaluation Strategies

Students apply a wide range of strategies to comprehend, interpret, evaluate, and appreciate texts. They draw on their prior experience, their interactions with other readers and writers, their knowledge of word meaning and of other texts, their word identification strategies, and their understanding of textual features (e.g., sound-letter correspondence, sentence structure, context, graphics). Students adjust their use of spoken, written, and visual language (e.g., conventions, style, vocabulary) to communicate effectively with a variety of audiences and for different purposes.

NL-ENG.K-12.12 Applying Language Skills

Students use spoken, written, and visual language to accomplish their own purpose (e.g., learning, enjoyment, persuasion, and the exchange of information).

Skills

- Comprehension

Grade Level: Third grade

Materials

- A collection of hats and boxes
- Small hat box for the questions
- Comprehension questions written on hats that have been copied onto construction paper and laminated
- Small flowers and ribbons to decorate the hats

Step 1: Introduce the title, author, and illustrator.

Step 2: Tell students to listen and be ready to answer questions at the conclusion of the story.

Step 3: Tell or read the story.

Step 4: Discuss the story.

Step 5: Divide class into twos.

Step 6: Give each group a question and give time for students to discuss their question. Students should remember the story without looking at the book.

Step 7: Each group reads their question and answer. Allow time for other students to comment on questions and disagree or agree with answers.

Comprehension Questions Labeled with Bloom's Levels of Thinking Taxonomy

Knowledge

When do Sarah and Susan visit Aunt Flossie?

What do Susan and Sarah eat first with Aunt Flossie?

What was one of Aunt Flossie's memories?

Comprehension

Describe the big parade.

Describe the fire in Baltimore.

Describe Aunt Flossie's house.

Application

Why do you think Sarah and Susan visit Aunt Flossie?

Why do you think Aunt Flossie allows the girls to play with her hats?

What state do you think Aunt Flossie lives in?

Do you think Aunt Flossie ate crab cakes long ago? Why or why not?

Share a memory from your family.

Analysis

Which one of Aunt Flossie's memories did you like the best? Why?

Synthesis

Describe another hat and memory as if you were Aunt Flossie.

Change the end of the story and choose another animal to rescue Aunt Flossie's special Sunday hat.

Evaluation

What was your favorite part?

What was the funniest part?

Aunt Flossie's Hats and Crab Cakes Later
By Elizabeth Fitzgerald Howard

Pattern

Look Out, Jack! The Giant Is Back!

by Tom Birdseye

Birdseye, Tom. *Look Out, Jack! The Giant Is Back!* New York: Holiday House, 2001.

Objective: Students will correctly answer the comprehension questions after the story.

Language Arts National Standards

NL-ENG.K-12.2 Understanding the Human Experience

Students read a wide range of literature from many periods in many genres to build an understanding of many dimensions (e.g., philosophical, ethical, aesthetic) of human experience.

NL-ENG.K-12.3 Evaluation Strategies

Students apply a wide range of strategies to comprehend, interpret, evaluate, and appreciate texts. They draw on their prior experience, their interactions with other readers and writers, their knowledge of word meaning and of other texts, their word identification strategies, and their understanding of textual features (e.g., sound-letter correspondence, sentence structure, context, graphics).

Skills

- Comprehension

Grade Level: Third grade

Materials

- Trace the foot of the giant from the story and cut out enough for each of the comprehension questions

Preparing Materials: Write out the comprehension questions on the giant feet and laminate. Label one of the extra feet the "Giant Feet Award."

Step 1: As the students enter, have them remove their shoes and sit in a circle for the story.

Step 2: Ask if students remember the story of Jack and the Beanstalk. Summarize the story with the help of the students.

Step 3: Read this new version of the story and share the pictures asking the students to listen for things that remind them of the other version.

Step 4: Lead the students in a discussion of the things that they remember about the original version of Jack and the Beanstalk. How did the author take those elements and create another story? Use the Venn diagram worksheet to compare and contrast these two versions.

Step 5: Use the comprehension questions for a face-off between the girls and the boys. Keep score on the board and rotate the questions until all have been answered.

Closure: Have students line up and measure their feet and award the one with the longest feet the "Giant Feet Award."

Comprehension Questions Labeled with Bloom's Levels of Thinking Taxonomy

Knowledge

Describe how Jack escapes to America.

Identify the state where Jack bought a farm.

What did Jack raise on his farm?

What color eyes did the giant have?

Describe the three things that the giant wanted from Jack and his mother.

List the things Jack and his mother made for the picnic.

Define the winner at the end of this tale.

Comprehension

Describe the giant in the story.

Compare this story to the original version and point out the similarities.

Compare this story to the original version and point out the differences.

Application

Estimate how tall the giant might have been. Example: He was twice my size.

Explain how the roses save the day.

Analysis

Which version of Jack did you enjoy the most? Justify your answer.

Synthesis

Change the ending of the story.

If you were writing another story about Jack, what trouble would he have in the next book?

Evaluation

Would you recommend this story to a friend? Why or why not?

Reading Resource Books

Harris, Jim. *Jack and the Giant: A Story Full of Beans*. Flagstaff, AZ: Rising Moon, 1997.

Kellogg, Steven. *Jack and the Beanstalk*. New York: Morrow Junior Books, 1991.

Osborne, Mary Pope. *Kate and the Beanstalk*. New York: Atheneum Books for Young Readers, 2000.

Venn Diagram Pattern

Old Version   **Look Out Jack!**

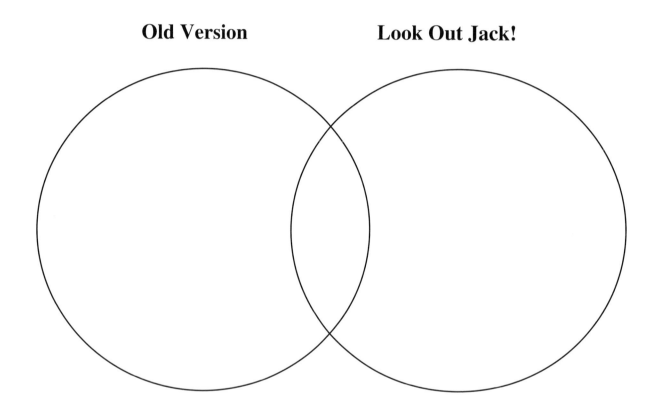

The Seven Silly Eaters

by Mary Ann Hoberman

Hoberman, Mary Ann. *The Seven Silly Eaters.* New York: Browndeer Press, 1997.

Objective: Students will correctly answer comprehension questions and write directions for a recipe after listening to the story.

Language Arts National Standards

NL-ENG.K-12.3 Evaluation Strategies

Students apply a wide range of strategies to comprehend, interpret, evaluate, and appreciate texts. They draw on their prior experience, their interactions with other readers and writers, their knowledge of word meaning and of other texts, their word identification strategies, and their understanding of textual features (e.g., sound-letter correspondence, sentence structure, context, graphics). Students adjust their use of spoken, written, and visual language (e.g., conventions, style, vocabulary) to communicate effectively with a variety of audiences and for different purposes.

NL-ENG.K-12.12 Applying Language Skills

Students use spoken, written, and visual language to accomplish their own purpose (e.g., learning, enjoyment, persuasion, and the exchange of information.

Skills

- Comprehension
- Writing directions

Grade Level: Third grade

Materials

- A sample cake recipe
- Worksheet copied for each student
- Comprehension questions written on index cards or recipe cards

Step 1: Introduce the title, author, and illustrator.

Step 2: Tell students they will be asked comprehension questions after the story has been read.

Step 3: Read story.

Step 4: Allow students to comment about illustrations and story.

Step 5: Students take turns reading and answering the questions.

Step 6: Show the sample cake recipe on the chalkboard. Read through the recipe with students. Talk about what items are included in a recipe (list of needed items and directions).

Step 7: With students' help, list foods the children used in the secret recipe in the story.

Step 8: Pass out the worksheet. Tell the students to write a recipe for the secret recipe in the story.

Step 9: Allow students time to complete their recipe.

Step 10: Students share their recipes.

Comprehension Questions Labeled with Bloom's Levels of Thinking Taxonomy

Knowledge

What activity was Mrs. Peters doing at the end of the story?

What activities were the children doing at the end of the story?

Comprehension

Summarize the beginning of the story.

Summarize the middle of the story.

Summarize the end of the story.

Application

What healthy foods were the children missing from their diets?

Synthesis

What other words could you substitute for "silly" in the title?

Evaluation

Explain how you or someone you know is a picky eater. What foods would that person not eat or only eat?

When you become a parent, how will you handle the eating habits of your children?

Have you ever tried to surprise a person on his or her birthday? Explain.

Teacher's Notes:

Here's what's cooking: _____

Recipe from: _____ Serves: _____

_____

_____

_____

_____

_____

_____

_____

_____

_____

_____

_____

_____

_____

_____

_____

_____

_____

_____

_____

The Blizzard

by Betty Ren Wright

Wright, Betty Ren. *The Blizzard*. New York: Holiday House, 2003.

Lesson 1

Objective: Students will correctly answer the questions at the end of the story.

Language Arts National Standards

NL-ENG.K-12.3 Evaluation Strategies

Students apply a wide range of strategies to comprehend, interpret, evaluate, and appreciate texts. They draw on their prior experience, their interactions with other readers and writers, their knowledge of word meaning and of other texts, their word identification strategies, and their understanding of textual features (e.g., sound-letter correspondence, sentence structure, context, graphics).

NL-ENG.K-12.4 Communication Skills

Students adjust their use of spoken, written, and visual language (e.g., conventions, style, vocabulary) to communicate effectively with a variety of audiences and for different purposes.

NL-ENG.K-12.12 Applying Language Skills

Students use spoken, written, and visual language to accomplish their own purpose (e.g., learning, enjoyment, persuasion, and the exchange of information.

NL-ENG.K-12.8 Developing Research Skills

Students use a variety of technological and informational resources (e.g., libraries, databases, computer networks, video) to gather and synthesize information and to create and communicate knowledge.

Skills

- Comprehension

Grade Level: Fourth grade

Materials

- Snowflakes cut from the die cut machine, if available
- Knit hat to hold the snowflakes
- White construction paper

46

Preparing Materials Write out the comprehension questions on construction paper, glue them onto the snowflakes, and laminate.

Step 1: Introduce the book and author. Ask the students to listen and see if this story reminds them of something similar that happened to them. Read the book and share the pictures as you read aloud.

Step 2: Use the comprehension questions at the end of the lesson to review the facts of the story. Call on students to draw a question out of the hat. If they have trouble answering, they can ask an expert from the audience to help provide the answer.

Closure: Allow some time for students to share personal snowstorm experiences.

Comprehension Questions Labeled with Bloom's Levels of Thinking Taxonomy

Knowledge

Who is having a birthday?

What special treat did Billy's mom send in his lunch?

What did she call this treat?

Describe what Billy's mom fixed for dinner.

What was served for dessert?

Make a list of the chores that the students helped with before supper.

Where did Miss Bailey sit for dinner?

Define "blizzard."

How did Billy's mom solve the problem of so many extra people for dinner?

Comprehension

Summarize the events at Billy's house

Contrast the events of a July birthday that Mae probably had with Billy's winter celebration. What would have been different?

Application

Estimate how many people ended up at Billy's house for supper. Justify your answer.

Analysis

How were Billy's feelings at the beginning of the story different from his feelings at the end? What changes took place?

Synthesis

Design an evening with your classmates if you were forced to stay at school because of bad weather.

Evaluation

Contrast your snowed-in evening at school with Billy's blizzard experience.

Lesson 2: Weather

Objective: Students answer the questions on the worksheet using the *USA TODAY* Web site.

NL-ENG.K-12.8 Developing Research Skills

Students use a variety of technological and informational resources (e.g., libraries, databases, computer networks, video) to gather and synthesize information and to create and communicate knowledge.

Skills

- Navigating a Web site

Materials

- Web site worksheet: http://www.usatoday.com/weather
- Worksheet about weather
- Nonfiction books about weather, dictionaries, and encyclopedias

Preparing Materials

- Visit the Web site and print out each step of the process of accessing the weather for a specific location. Make these copies into overheads.
- On the worksheets, put the name of a different state on each student copy so that different students report on different states. Create a display of weather-related books, dictionaries, encyclopedias, and magazines.

Step 1: Hand out the worksheets and introduce the lesson by asking what kind of weather was talked about in *The Blizzard.*

Step 2: Using the overheads explain the process of looking up the weather for the day using the Web site.

Step 3: Read through the steps with the students.

Step 4: Explain that students will take turns looking up the answers to the weather worksheet questions while the remaining members of the class look up facts about blizzards. Students will use the resources to find facts about blizzards.

Step 5: Divide the class, depending on the number of computers available. Some students will work with the computers, and others will work on the weather fact worksheet using books and other materials.

Step 6: Rotate groups until all have finished.

Reading Resource Books

Erlbach, Arlene. *Blizzards.* Chicago: Children's Press, 1995.

Haslam, Andrew, and Barbara Taylor. *Weather.* Chicago: World Book, 1997.

Simon, Seymour. *Weather.* New York: Morrow Junior Books, 1993.

Weather Web Site
http://www.usatoday.com/weather

Name:_____

Directions:

Step 1: Connect to the Internet.

Step 2: Click on the current Web address and delete.

Step 3: Type the weather address Web site in that space.

Step 4: Click on the "go" button or press the return key.

Step 5: Find Forecasts on the left side of the screen.

Step 6: Click on U.S. locations.

Step 7: Find your state and click on the name.

Step 8: Click on one of the cities listed at the top of the screen.

Answer the following:

Name of the state:_____

City: _____

Record Temperatures:

High _____ Low _____

Sunrise _____

Sunset _____

What is the predicted weather for tomorrow? _____

From *Using Picture Books to Teach Language Arts Standards in Grades 3–5*, written and illustrated by Brenda S. Copeland and Patricia A. Messner. Westport, CT: Libraries Unlimited. Copyright © 2006.

Weather Worksheet

Answer the following questions about weather. You will need to use the dictionary, encyclopedias, and other resources.

1. Look up the word "meteorologist" in the dictionary. Write out the definition and then use the word in a sentence.

   _____

   _____

   _____

   _____

2. Look up "weather" in the encyclopedia and list four types of storms.

   _____   _____

   _____   _____

3. List some pieces of equipment that are used to observe the weather.

   _____

   _____

   _____

   _____

4. Describe the weather today in your neighborhood. Use complete sentences.

   _____

   _____

   _____

   _____

The Lady in the Box

by Ann McGovern

McGovern, Ann. *The Lady in the Box.* New York: Turtle Books, 1997.

Objective: Students will correctly answer comprehension questions after listening to the story.

Language Arts National Standards

NL-ENG.K-12.3 Evaluation Strategies

Students apply a wide range of strategies to comprehend, interpret, evaluate, and appreciate texts. They draw on their prior experience, their interactions with other readers and writers, their knowledge of word meaning and of other texts, their word identification strategies, and their understanding of textual features (e.g., sound-letter correspondence, sentence structure, context graphics).

NL-ENG.K-12.12 Applying Language Skills

Students use spoken, written, and visual language to accomplish their own purpose (e.g., for learning, enjoyment, persuasion, and the exchange of information).

Skills

- Comprehension

Grade Level: Fourth grade

Materials

- Comprehension questions written on the box pattern on brown construction paper and laminated
- Worksheet for each student
- Pencils
- Small brown box for questions

Preparing Materials: Using the box pattern on the worksheet (enlarge as needed), cut out boxes from brown construction paper, write comprehension questions on them, and laminate.

Step 1: Introduce the title, author, and subject. Show the cover and ask students what they think the book is about. Allow time for answers and comments.

Step 2: Read story. Allow time for comments and predictions.

Step 3: Students take turns selecting and answering the questions from the box.

Step 4: Pass out worksheets and pencils. Explain the directions and allow time for the completion of the worksheet.

Step 5: Gather students back together and share worksheet.

Comprehension Questions Labeled with Bloom's Levels of Thinking Taxonomy

Knowledge

Why did the lady sleep in a box?

What did Lizzie and her brother give the lady in the box?

What was the lady's name?

Comprehension

Describe the setting and time of year.

Compare the lady's life and the lives of Lizzie and her brother.

Application

What are some words you could use to describe Lizzie and her brother's actions?

Analysis

What was the saddest part?

What was your favorite part?

Synthesis

What would you have done if you were Lizzie and her brother?

How can or how has our school helped people who are in need?

Teacher's Notes:

Write the many things you own that are in your house on the space outside the box. Inside the box write only the things you could fit in a stove box.

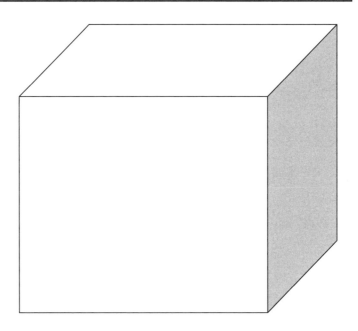

Thinking Question:

Describe what you would do each day if you lived in a box. Include where you would put the box during the day and how you would carry your things during the day.

_____

_____

_____

_____

_____

_____

The Purple Coat

by Amy Hest

Hest, Amy. *The Purple Coat.* New York: Four Winds Press, 1986.

Objective: Students will listen to a story, answer comprehension questions correctly, and write a personal experience narrative about how they have asked for something.

Language Arts National Standards

NL-Eng.K-12.3 Evaluation Strategies

Students apply a wide range of strategies to comprehend, interpret, evaluate, and appreciate texts. They draw on their prior experience, their interactions with other readers and writers, their knowledge of word meaning and of other texts, their word identification strategies, and their understanding of textual features (e.g., sound-letter correspondence, sentence structure, context, graphics).

NL-ENG.K-12.12 Applying Language Skills

Students use spoken, written, and visual language to accomplish their own purpose (e.g., learning, enjoyment, persuasion, and the exchange of information.

Skills

- Comprehension
- Writing

Grade Level: Fourth grade

Materials

- Blue and purple construction paper
- Pattern for coat
- Rubber cement
- Old buttons
- Permanent marker

Preparing Materials: Cut out coats from construction paper. Offset a purple coat with a blue coat and glue together. The blue coat should be on the bottom and the purple coat on top. Write questions on the purple coats, laminate, and glue an old button on the center of the purple coat.

Step 1: Introduce the title, author, and illustrator. Tell students they will be asked to answer comprehension questions after the reading of the story.

Step 2: Read the story and allow time for students to comment on the story.

Step 3: Students take turns reading and answering the questions.

Step 4: With the help of the students, list how Gabby convinced her grandfather and mother to make her a purple coat instead of a navy coat.

Step 5: Pass out the worksheets. Read the directions with the students.

Step 6: Allow time for students to complete the worksheets.

Step 7: Students share their worksheets.

Comprehension Questions Labeled with Bloom's Levels of Thinking Taxonomy

Knowledge

What was Grandpa's occupation?

What kind of food did Gabby and Grandpa enjoy when Gabby visited?

Where did Mother go when Gabby and Grandpa measured Gabby for the new coat?

Comprehension

Summarize the problem.

Describe the subway.

Summarize the solution.

Describe Grandpa's desk.

Application

How would you change the end of the story and the title?

Analysis

What is the funniest part of the story?

What was your favorite part of the story?

Synthesis

What choice would you have made if you were the grandfather?

Evaluation

Where do you think Gabby and her mother lived?

Where do you think Grandpa's tailor shop was located?

Describe an experience when you asked for something and were told no because you have always done it another way.

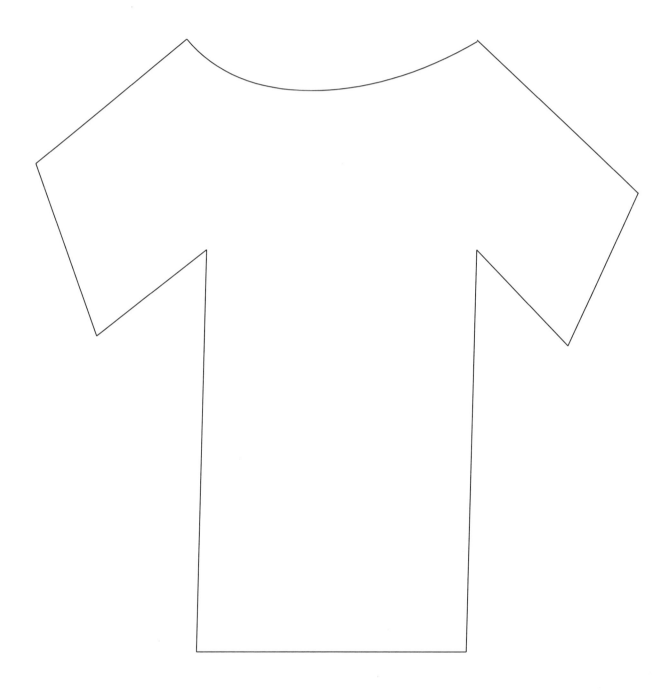

Write a request for something new or different. Include reasons for needing the new or different item.

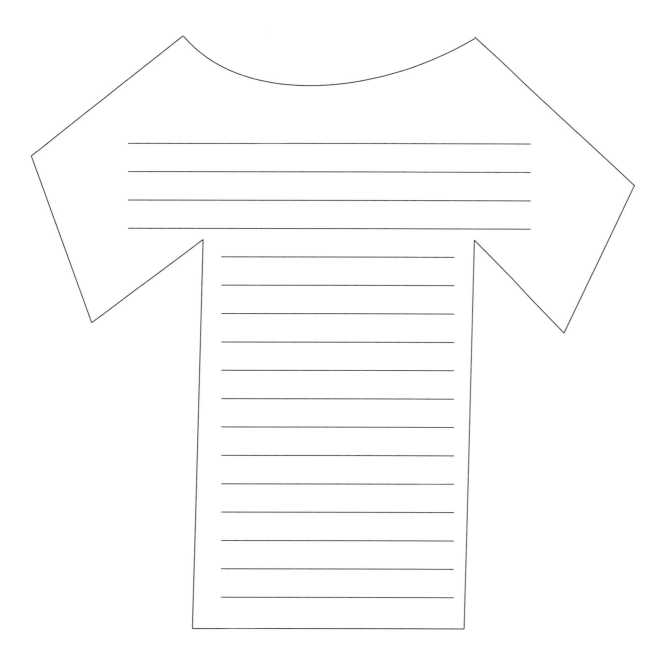

Shoeless Joe & Black Betty

by Phil Bildner

Bildner, Phil. *Shoeless Joe & Black Betty*. New York: Simon & Schuster for Young Readers, 2002.

Objective: Students will correctly answer the comprehension questions after reading the story.

Language Arts National Standards

NL-ENG.K-12.2 Understanding the Human Experience

Students read a wide range of literature from many periods in many genres to build an understanding of many dimensions (e.g., philosophical, ethical, aesthetic) of human experience.

NL-ENG.K-12.3 Evaluation Strategies

Students apply a wide range of strategies to comprehend, interpret, evaluate, and appreciate texts. They draw on their prior experience, their interactions with other readers and writers, their knowledge of word meaning and of other texts, their word identification strategies, and their understanding of textual features (e.g., sound-letter correspondence, sentence structure, context, graphics).

Skills

- Comprehension

Grade Level: Fourth grade

Materials

- Round circles cut from white construction paper

- Baseball cap from your favorite team and an old bat

Preparing Materials: Write out the comprehension questions on circles.

Step 1: Introduce the lesson by asking what are the favorite teams of the class. Make a list on the board. Ask what kind of problems a baseball player might have.

Step 2: Ask the students to listen for the problem that Joe Jackson had in regard to his game performance. Read the story and share the pictures.

Step 3: Place the questions in the hat you are wearing and call on students to draw a question from that hat and read it to the class. Allow time for discussion because some of the questions will require more thought.

Closure: End the lesson by stressing how Joe solved the problem of not being able to hit the ball. Discuss what the real problem was. Was it a problem with the bat as much as it was just staying with the task and practicing until he was good at batting? Use the worksheet as an extra writing activity. Each student should think of something that he or she really wants to do and plan steps for accomplishing this goal.

Comprehension Questions Labeled with Bloom's Levels of Thinking Taxonomy

Knowledge

Where did Joe Jackson get his nickname?

Describe what Joe tried to do to improve his hitting.

Name the friend to whom Joe always kept going back to for help.

List the times that Joe was sent back to the minors.

What was the name of Joe's bat.

Describe the technique Joe used to take care of his bat.

In what part of the country was Joe born (north, south, east, or west)?

Identify the wood used for the bat.

Name the teams for which Joe played.

Define the process used to turn the bat black.

What other famous player copied Joe's swing?

Comprehension

Summarize Joe Jackson's career in baseball.

Defend Joe's view that he needed a better bat when things went wrong.

Application

What did you learn from Joe Jackson's life?

Does this story remind you of a time when you tried to play a game and didn't do as well as you might have? How did you solve the problem?

Analysis

What words would you use to describe how Joe felt when he was sent back to the minors?

Synthesis

Tell the story from the bat's point of view.

Pretend you have just signed on Joe Jackson as part of your new baseball team. Compose a news release that supports your actions.

Evaluation

Explain why Joe is important to baseball. Justify your answer.

Reading Resource Books

Aaseng, Nathan. *Sports Great Kirby Puckett*. Berkeley Heights, NJ: Enslow, 1993.

Adler, David A. *Lou Gehrig: The Luckiest Man*. New York: Harcourt Books, 1997.

Breitenbucher, Cathy. *Bonnie Blair*. Minneapolis, MN: Lerner, 1994.

Think about how Joe Jackson became a great ball player and make a list in the box.
What do you dream of being able to do when you grow up? Write your dream on the baseball and explain how you will accomplish this task on the inside of the bat.

My dream

Joe Jackson became a great ball player because

1. _____

_____

2. _____

_____

3. _____

_____

My plan

Pink and Say

by Patricia Polacco

Polacco, Patricia. *Pink and Say*. New York: Philomel Books, 1994.

Lesson 1

Objective: Students will correctly answer the questions at the end of the story and locate the related words in the dictionary and use them in a sentence.

Language Arts National Standards

NL-ENG.K-12.3 Evaluation Strategies

Students apply a wide range of strategies to comprehend, interpret, evaluate, and appreciate texts. They draw on their prior experience, their interactions with other readers and writers, their knowledge of word meaning and of other texts, their word identification strategies, and their understanding of textual features (e.g., sound-letter correspondence, sentence structure, context, graphics).

NL-ENG.K-12.4 Communication Skills

Students adjust their use of spoken, written, and visual language (e.g., conventions, style, vocabulary) to communicate effectively with a variety of audiences and for different purposes.

NL-ENG.K-12.12 Applying Language Skills

Students use spoken, written, and visual language to accomplish their own purpose (e.g., learning, enjoyment, persuasion, and the exchange of information.

Skills

- Comprehension
- Dictionary skills

Grade Level: Fifth grade

Materials

- Dictionary worksheet
- Dictionaries for the class

Step 1: Introduce the story by asking students to listen for signs of bravery.

Step 2: Read the story and share the pictures as you read.

Step 3: Use the comprehension questions at the end of the lesson to review the details of the story.

Step 4: Direct the students to turn to a partner and explain who was brave in this story and why. Bring students back together and have a brief discussion about this topic.

Closure: Hand out the worksheet and go over the directions for the dictionary practice.

Comprehension Questions Labeled with Bloom's Levels of Thinking Taxonomy

Knowledge

From what state was Sheldon?

What did "Flying Union Colors" mean?

What was the name of the company with which Pinkus Aylee fought?

What was Sheldon's nickname?

Why did Pinkus have the same last name as his master?

Why did Pinkus bless the house where his master lived?

Explain what Sheldon was proud to say he had been able to accomplish.

Describe what Pinkus meant by the "sickness."

Where did Moe Moe Bay hide the boys when the marauders came?

Why did Pinkus give Sheldon his spectacles?

Comprehension

Contrast the lives of the two boys. How were they different?

Summarize the events at Pinkus Aylee's house when Say was recovering from his wounds.

Application

Calculate how many days it took for the boys to rest and recover.

After hearing this story, would one boy be considered a coward? Justify your answer.

Analysis

Outline the main events in the story.

What was the saddest part in the book? Defend your answer.

Synthesis

What would have happened if the Rebel Army had not picked up the boys?

If the roles were reversed and Pinkus had been wounded, would the story's plot have changed? Would Sheldon have befriended Pinkus in the same manner?

Evaluation

Pinkus and Sheldon both fought for the Union Army. Which side would you have fought to preserve? Explain your answer.

Lesson 2: Internet Activity

Objective: Students will research the Medal of Honor and write a letter persuading the president of the United States to give Pinkus this medal.

Language Arts National Standards

NL-ENG.K-12.7 Evaluating Data

Students conduct research on issues and interest by generating ideas and questions, and by posing problems. They gather, evaluate, and synthesize data from a variety of sources (e.g., print and nonprint texts, artifacts, people) to communicate their discoveries in ways that suit their purpose and audience.

NL-ENG.K-12.8 Developing Research Skills

Students use a variety of technological and information resources (e.g., libraries, databases, computer networks, video) to gather and synthesize information and to create and communicate knowledge.

NL-ENG.K-12.12 Applying Language Skills

Students use spoken, written, and visual language to accomplish their own purpose (e.g., learning, enjoyment, persuasion, and the exchange of information.

Skills

- Research on the Internet

Grade Level: Fifth grade

Materials

- Scrap paper for note taking
- Pencils
- Paper for both rough copy and final letter copy
- Star overhead

Preparing Materials: Write the following questions on the board for easy access to students:

- Why is the Medal of Honor given?
- During what war was the medal first given and why?
- Who is the latest recipient?

Step 1: Review the story from Lesson 1.

Step 2: Using the overhead, brainstorm characteristics of bravery. Write them on the points of the star.

Step 3: Divide students into groups depending on the number of computers in your library media center. Some students can find books on the shelves about the Civil War while they wait to access the Web site.

Step 4: Allow time for students to complete the task and then ask them to report back to the group so that everyone can answer the questions on the board.

Closure: Explain the following writing assignment and hand out papers:

Pretend you are Sheldon Russell Curtis and write a letter of recommendation that would persuade President Lincoln to give Pinkus Aylee the Congressional Medal of Honor.

Resources

Wachet, Roger. *The Medal of Honor*. New York: Children's Press, 2002.

The World Book Encyclopedia. Chicago: World Book.

Congressional Medal of Honor: www.cmohs.org

Reading Resource Books

Brewer, Paul. *The American Civil War*. Austin, TX: Raintree Steck-Vaughn, 1999.

Bunting, Eve. *The Blue and the Gray*. New York: Scholastic, 1996.

Erdosh, George. *Food and Recipes of the Civil War*. New York: PowerKids Press, 1997.

Hite, Sid. *The Journal of Rufus Rowe: A Witness to the Battle of Fredericksburg*. New York: Scholastic, 2003.

Teacher's Notes:

Dictionary Worksheet

Look up the following words in the dictionary. Write out definitions that would apply to this story, and use the words in a sentence.

1. marauders _____

_____

_____

2. spectacles _____

_____

_____

_____

3. quartered _____

_____

_____

_____

4. buckboard _____

_____

_____

_____

5. mahogany _____

_____

_____

_____

6. slaughtered _____

_____

_____

_____

7. ransacked _____

_____

_____

_____

Characteristics of Bravery

The Rag Coat

by Lauren Mills

Mills, Lauren. *The Rag Coat*. New York: Little, Brown & Company, 1991.

Objective: Students will answer the comprehension questions and complete the worksheet on problem solving.

Language Arts National Standards

NL-ENG.K-12.2 Understanding the Human Experience

Students read a wide range of literature from many periods in many genres to build an understanding of many dimensions (e.g., philosophical, ethical, aesthetic) of human experience.

NL-ENG.K-12.3 Evaluation Strategies

Students apply a wide range of strategies to comprehend, interpret, evaluate, and appreciate texts. They draw on their prior experience, their interactions with other readers and writers, their knowledge of word meaning and of other texts, their word identification strategies, and their understanding of textual features (e.g., sound-letter correspondence, sentence structure, context, graphics).

Skills

- Comprehension

Grade Level: Fifth grade

Materials

- Flannel board
- Fifteen square felt pieces (3 or 4 inches square)
- An old quilt

Preparing Materials: Write out the comprehension questions on white paper and pin or glue them to the felt squares.

Step 1: Spread the quilt on the floor and invite students to sit around the edges for the lesson.

Step 2: As you start the lesson, you might explain that sometimes quilt pieces can tell a story about a family. Introduce the book and author. Explain to students that quilting is an important part of this story.

Step 3: Read the story.

Step 4: As the students answer the comprehension questions on the felt squares, place the squares on the flannel board to form a quilt pattern.

Closure: Pass out the worksheet and go over the directions. Allow time for individual work. Share problems and solutions if possible.

Comprehension Questions Labeled with Bloom's Levels of Thinking Taxonomy

Knowledge

Identify the setting of this story.

Why can't Minna go to school?

Describe how Minna's dad keeps her warm when they ride in the wagon.

Define the term "feed sack."

Describe how the burlap felt.

Identify what is wrong with Minna's dad.

How does Minna's mom bring money to the household accounts?

Comprehension

Describe the school.

Explain what Minna's dad meant by "people only need people, and nothing else."

Application

Calculate how long it took the quilting mothers to finish the rag coat. Justify your answer.

Does this story remind you of a time when your classmates made fun of you? Explain.

Analysis

Clarify the hardest thing that Minna had to do.

Synthesis

Tell the story from Shane's point of view.

Explain why family stories are important.

Evaluation

Look critically at the classroom behavior at the beginning and end of the story. How did it change? Does this remind you of how we should treat others? Support your reasoning with examples.

Reading Resource Books

Cobb, Mary. *The Quilt-Block History of Pioneer Days: With Projects Kids Can Make.* Brookfield, CT: Millbrook Press, 1995.

Polacco, Patricia. *The Keeping Quilt.* New York: Simon & Schuster Books for Young Readers, 1988.

Smucker, Barbara C. *Selina and the Shoo-fly Pie.* New York: Stoddart Kids, 1999.

Turner, Ann Warren. *Sewing Quilts.* New York: Macmillan, 1994.

Vaughan, Marcia K. *The Secret to Freedom.* New York: Lee & Low Books, 2001.

Does this story remind you of a difficult situation in your classroom? Map out a plan to solve this problem using the nine-patch quilt block.

Person I have the problem with.	**Step 2**	People who helped me solve this problem.
Step 1	**Describe the Problem**	**Step 4**
Place where problem takes place.	**Step 3**	How do I feel when the problem is solved?

Sister Anne's Hands

by Marybeth Lorbiecki

Lorbiecki, Marybeth. *Sister Anne's Hands*. New York: Dial Books for Young Readers, 1998.

Objective: Students will correctly answer the comprehension questions after the story and complete the worksheet about a favorite teacher.

Language Arts National Standards

NL-ENG.K-12.2 Understanding the Human Experience

Students read a wide range of literature from many periods in many genres to build an understanding of many dimensions (e.g., philosophical, ethical, aesthetic) of human experience.

NL-ENG.K-12.3 Evaluation Strategies

Students apply a wide range of strategies to comprehend, interpret, evaluate, and appreciate texts. They draw on their prior experience, their interactions with other readers and writers, their knowledge of word meaning and of other texts, their word identification strategies, and their understanding of textual features (e.g., sound-letter correspondence, sentence structure, context, graphics).

Skills

- Comprehension
- Writing a paragraph

Grade Level: Fifth grade

Materials

- Fifteen hands cut from a variety of colored construction paper

Preparing Materials: Write out the comprehension questions on white paper and glue them to the hands.

Step 1: Introduce the story by explaining that this story takes place in the 1960s. Explain a little about what the 1960s were like. Ask students to listen for ways that the main character changes during the story.

Step 2: Read the story and share the pictures.

Step 3: Lead the students in a discussion about the changes they saw in the main character.

Step 4: Pass out the questions so that every pair of students has a question.

Step 5: Allow a few minutes for the students to talk about the answers with their partners. Take turns with the student pairs reading the questions and answers and having the class decide whether the answer is correct.

Closure: Follow up with the worksheet. Go over the directions and model an example for the students.

Comprehension Questions Labeled with Bloom's Levels of Thinking Taxonomy

Knowledge

Identify what grade Anna is in at school and the kind of school she attended.

Describe the activities that Anna's class did that made learning fun.

List some famous people about whom Sister Anne taught the students and recall why they are famous.

Where was Sister Anne teaching by the start of the next year?

How old was Anna in the story?

Why was Anna afraid of the new teacher?

Comprehension

Why did some people not like the new teacher?

Explain why Anna decided to draw hands that were different colors as a good-bye present for Sister Anne.

Generalize what important lesson Anna learned in second grade. Justify your answer.

Application

Does this story remind you of a special teacher? Explain why this teacher is so special.

What does hate look like? Have you ever seen this at your school? Can we change hate?

Analysis

Outline the main events in this story.

Clarify why some parents pulled their children out of the class.

Synthesis

At the end of the story, Anna will be in third grade. What problems might Anna encounter?

Evaluation

Does hate have a color? What is it and why?

Reading Resource Books

Gregson, Susan R. *Phillis Wheatley*. Mankato, MN: Bridgestone Books, 2002.

Hill, Kirkpatrick. *The Year of Miss Agnes*. New York: Margaret K. McElderry, 2000.

Selden, Bernice. *The Story of Annie Sullivan: Helen Keller's Teacher*. Milwaukee, WI: Gareth Stevens, 1997.

Wittman, Sally. *The Wonderful Mrs. Trumbly*. New York: Harper & Row, 1982.

Which Teacher Is Special in Your Life?

Decide which teacher reminds you of Sister Anne. Draw your hand in the box below. Write that teacher's name on the palm of your hand and write something that supports your claim on each of the fingers. Turn the paper over and then use those supporting ideas to create a paragraph that answers the question, "Which teacher is special in my life?"

Part Three

Story Elements
Favorites

Muncha! Muncha! Muncha!

by Candace Fleming

Fleming, Candace. *Muncha! Muncha! Muncha!* New York: Atheneum Books for Young Readers, 2002.

Objective: Students will identify the story elements and write a summary.

Language Arts National Standards

NL-ENG.K-12.1 Reading for Perspective

Students read a wide range of print and nonprint texts to build understanding of texts, of themselves, and of the cultures of the United States and the world; to acquire new information; to respond to the needs and demands of society and the workplace; and for personal fulfillment. Among these texts are fiction and nonfiction, classic and contemporary works.

NL-ENG.K-12.3 Evaluation Strategies

Students apply a wide range of strategies to comprehend, interpret, evaluate, and appreciate texts. They draw on their prior experience, their interactions with other readers and writers, their knowledge of word meaning and of other texts, their word identification strategies, and their understanding of textual features (e.g., sound-letter correspondence, sentence structure, context, graphics).

Skills

- Story elements
- Writing a summary

Materials

- Seven packs of seeds prepared with story elements
- Magnetic board
- Garden signs
- Worksheet copied for each student
- Pencils

Preparing Materials: Create the signs and stakes (make four copies of the garden sign pattern included here; write one of the following words on each sign: *characters, setting, problem,* and *solution*; laminate the signs). For the stakes, take a wire coat hanger and cut and bend to form the stakes. Tape stakes to the backs of the signs. Glue magnets on the backs of the signs.

Copy, cut out, and laminate the second set of patterns. Glue these to the outsides of the seed packets. There should be seven seed packets: one for each of the four characters, one for the setting, one for the problem, and one for the solution. Glue magnets on the backs of the seed packets.

Step 1: Place garden signs on the magnetic board.

Step 2: Introduce the story, author, and illustrator.

Step 3: Tell students to listen for the characters, setting, problem, and solution. Read the story.

Step 4: Pass out seed packets you have prepared ahead of time. Ask students to place their seed packets under the correct garden signs.

Step 5: Pass out the worksheets and pencils. Tell students that they will write a summary using the information on the magnetic board. Allow time for students to write a summary.

Step 6: Share summaries.

Teacher's Notes:

Garden Sign Pattern

Mr. McGreely

Rabbit 1

Rabbit 2

Rabbit 3

Mr. McGreely's Garden

The rabbits were eating Mr. McGreely's vegetables.

Mr. McGreely locked his garden. The rabbits hid in Mr. McGreely's basket. Mr. McGreely and the rabbits shared the vegetables.

Muncha! Muncha! Muncha
By Candace Fleming

Worksheet

Tacky and the Emperor

by Helen Lester

Lester, Helen. *Tacky and the Emperor.* Boston: Houghton Mifflin, 2000.

Objective: Students will recall and write the characters, setting, problem, and solution.

Language Arts National Standards

NL-ENG.K-12.1 Reading for Perspective

Students read a wide range of print and nonprint texts to build understanding of texts, of themselves, and of the cultures of the United States and the world; to acquire new information; to respond to the needs and demands of society and the workplace; and for personal fulfillment. Among these texts are fiction and nonfiction, classic and contemporary works.

NL-ENG.K-12.3 Evaluation Strategies

Students apply a wide range of strategies to comprehend, interpret, evaluate, and appreciate texts. They draw on their prior experience, their interactions with other readers and writers, their knowledge of word meaning and of other texts, their word identification strategies, and their understanding of textual features (e.g., sound-letter correspondence, sentence structure, context, graphics).

Skills

- Story elements

Grade Level: Third grade

Materials

- Worksheet copied for each student

- Pencils

- Chalkboard or dry erase board

Step 1: Introduce the title, author and illustrator. Review characters, setting, problem, and solution. Talk about a familiar story such as "The Three Little Pigs." Have students pick out the story elements from that story. Tell students to listen for the characters, setting, problem, and solution as you read *Tacky and the Emperor.*

Step 2: Read the story and allow time for student comments.

Step 3: Pass out worksheets and pencils. Read the directions for the worksheet with students. Allow time for the students to complete the worksheets.

Step 4: Students share worksheets. Write their answers on the chalkboard or dry erase board. Allow time for students to make corrections on their worksheets.

Write the character names, the setting, the problem, and the solution on the blocks of ice.

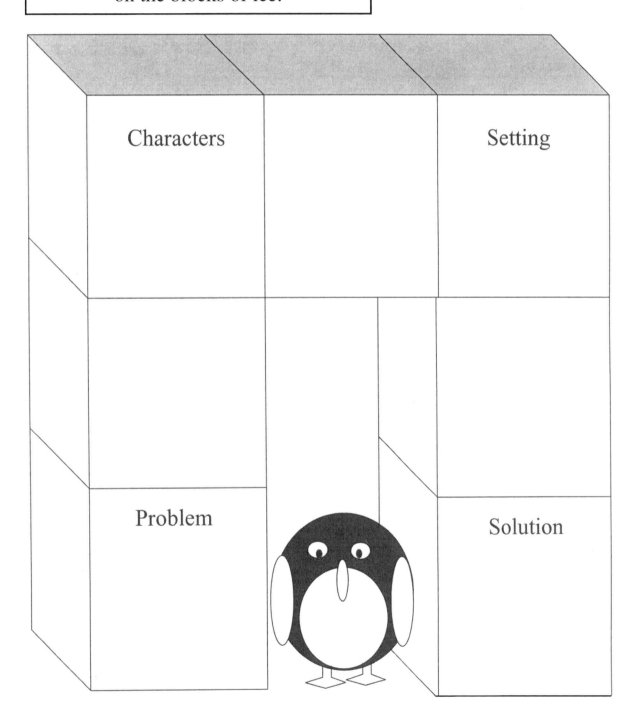

Characters

Setting

Problem

Solution

Bigfoot Cinderrrrrella

by Tony Johnson

Johnston, Tony. *Bigfoot Cinderrrrella*. New York: Putnam, 1998.

Objective: Students will compare *Bigfoot Cinderrrrella* to other versions of the Cinderella story and point out story elements that differ.

Language Arts National Standards

NL-ENG.K-12.1 Reading for Perspective

Students read a wide range of print and nonprint texts to build an understanding of texts, of themselves, and of the cultures of the United States and the world; to acquire new information; to respond to the needs and demands of society and the workplace; and for personal fulfillment. Among these texts are fiction and nonfiction, classic and contemporary works.

NL-ENG.K-12.3 Evaluation Strategies

Students apply a wide range of strategies to comprehend, interpret, evaluate, and appreciate texts. They draw on their prior experience, their interactions with other readers and writers, their knowledge of word meaning and of other texts, their word identification strategies, and their understanding of textual features (e.g., sound-letter correspondence, sentence structure, context, graphics).

Skills

- Story elements
- Text-to-text story comparison

Grade Level: Fourth grade

Materials

- Worksheet for each group
- Collection of Cinderella stories (see list at the end of the lesson)
- Magic wand and crown

Step 1: Introduce the lesson by explaining that many cultures and countries have a Cinderella story. This one is a newer version, but it has some of the same elements as the older stories. Depending on your class, you may need to spend time talking about the following elements in fairy tales. Who has magical powers? What kind of shoe is used? Does the author use the number three in the story? Do the characters live happily ever after? What kind of party or ball do they have? As you read the story, have the students listen for the elements that are different from the version with which they are most familiar.

Step 2: Put on the crown and read the story.

Step 3: Briefly discuss what the students remember after hearing the story. Ask key questions if needed. Example: Who has magical powers? How were the characters different? Make a chart on the board so that the students can see the things that are different between the Bigfoot Cinderella and the original one.

Bigfoot Cinderella	Cinderella

Step 4: Divide the class into groups depending on the number of Cinderella stories you have in your collection. Check the list of books at the end of the lesson for suggestions. Each group will need a worksheet and a Cinderella story. They will need to read and compare the version with the Bigfoot story using the worksheet as a guide.

Closure: After giving the groups time to complete the assignment, return to the main group and give each group time to share and compare.

Reading Resource Books

Climo, Shirley. *The Persian Cinderella*. New York: HarperCollins, 1999.

Climo, Shirley. *The Egyptian Cinderella*. New York: Harper Trophy, 1989.

Hickox, Rebecca. *The Golden Sandal: A Middle Eastern Cinderella Story*. New York: Holiday House, 1998.

Jackson, Ellen B. *Cinder Edna*. New York: Lothrop, Lee & Shepard, 1994.

Louie, Ai-Ling. *Yeh-Shen: A Cinderella Story from China*. New York: Philomel, 1982.

Lowell, Susan. *Cindy Ellen: A Wild Western Cinderella*. New York: HarperCollins, 2000.

Martin, Rafe. *The Rough-Face Girl*. New York: G.P. Putnam's Sons, 1992.

Schroeder, Alan. *Smoky Mountain Rose: An Appalachian Cinderella*. New York: Dial Books for Young Readers, 1997.

Teacher's Notes:

Worksheet

Read a second Cinderella story with the others in your group. Compare *Bigfoot Cinderrrrrella* to the story. Record your findings in the spaces below.

What is the name of the book your group read? _____

_____

	Bigfoot Cinderella	_____Cinderella
Main Character		
Supporting Characters		
Party or ball?		
Ending of story		
Type of shoe		
Who has magical powers?		

From *Using Picture Books to Teach Language Arts Standards in Grades 3–5*, written and illustrated by Brenda S. Copeland and Patricia A. Messner. Westport, CT: Libraries Unlimited. Copyright © 2006.

The Christmas Miracle of Jonathan Toomey

by Susan Wojciechowski

Wojciechowski, Susan. *The Christmas Miracle of Jonathan Toomey.* Cambridge, MA: Candlewick Press, 1995.

Objective: Students will identify the story elements and become familiar with a Web site.

Language Arts National Standards

NL-ENG.K-12.1 Reading for Perspective

Students read a wide range of print and nonprint texts to build an understanding of texts, of themselves, and of the cultures of the United States and the world; to acquire new information; to respond to the needs and demands of society and the workplace; and for personal fulfillment. Among these texts are fiction and nonfiction, classic and contemporary works.

NL-ENG.K-12.3 Evaluation Strategies

Students apply a wide range of strategies to comprehend, interpret, evaluate, and appreciate texts. They draw on their prior experience, their interactions with other readers and writers, their knowledge of word meaning and of other texts, their word identification strategies, and their understanding of textual features (e.g., sound-letter correspondence, sentence structure, context, graphics).

Skills

- Story elements
- Writing a summary
- Navigating a Web site

Grade Level: Fourth grade

Materials

- Two pieces of red felt
- Black puffy paint
- Large index cards
- Pencils
- Water-based markers
- Scissors
- Easel or chalkboard

Preparing Materials: Cut felt pieces in half. Fringe ends of the pieces of felt, making it resemble the scarf in the story. Write each of the following words with puffy paint on one piece of felt: *characters, setting, problem, solution.*

Step 1: Introduce the title, author, and illustrator. Tell students to listen for the characters, setting, problem, and solution as the story is read. Place felt pieces on the easel or chalkboard.

Step 2: Read the story.

Step 3: Discuss story.

Step 4: Divide the class into four groups. Give each group a large index card, a pencil, and a water-based marker.

Step 5: Assign each group a story element. The group writes one of the following words in pencil on one side of the card: *characters, setting, problem,* or *solution.* Each group is assigned an element, discusses the element, and then writes a complete sentence describing the element on the other side of the card.

Step 6: Add cards to board and read the summary.

Web Site Worksheet

Susan Wojciechowski's Web Site
http://goose.ycp.edu/~swojciec/

Name: _____

Directions:

     Step 1: Log onto the Internet.
     Step 2: Click on the current Web address.
     Step 3: Type the Web address above.
     Step 4: Click on the "go" button or press the return key.
     Step 5: Answer questions using the Web site.

1. Find another book written by Susan Wojciechowski and write it below.

_____

2. Find a "cool" link, go to that link, and write the Web address below.

_____

3. Find three interesting facts about Susan Wojciechowski.

     1. _____

     2. _____

     3. _____

4. Find your favorite bookmarked site and write its name on the line.

_____

5. Besides reading, what two other things does Susan like to do?

1. _____ 2. _____

Gullywasher Gulch

by Marianne Mitchell

Mitchell, Marianne. *Gullywasher Gulch.* Honesdale, PA: Boyds Mills Press, 2002.

Objective: Students will listen to the story, identify the story elements and idioms, and look up idioms in a thesaurus.

Language Arts National Standards

NL-ENG.K-12.1 Reading for Perspective

Students read a wide range of print and nonprint texts to build understanding of texts, of themselves, and of the cultures of the United States and the world; to acquire new information; to respond to the needs and demands of society and the workplace; and for personal fulfillment. Among these texts are fiction and nonfiction, classic and contemporary works.

NL-ENG.K-12.3 Evaluation Strategies

Students apply a wide range of strategies to comprehend, interpret, evaluate, and appreciate texts. They draw on their prior experience, their interactions with other readers and writers, their knowledge of word meaning and of other texts, their word identification strategies, and their understanding of textual features (e.g., sound-letter correspondence, sentence structure, context, graphics).

NL-ENG.K-12.9 Multicultural Understanding

Students develop an understanding of and respect for diversity in language use, patterns, and dialects across cultures, ethic groups, geographic regions, and social roles.

Skills

- Story elements
- Idioms

Grade Level: Fourth grade

Materials

- Worksheet copied for each student
- Dictionaries and dictionaries of idioms—examples:
  - Terabn, Marvin. *Dictionary of Idioms.* New York: Scholastic, 1996.
  - *Webster's Dictionary and Thesaurus.* Scotland: Geddes & Grosset, 2002.
- Pencils

Step 1: Introduce the title, author, and illustrator. Tell students to listen for the story elements and idioms. If needed, review the definition of an idiom and show examples of common idioms.

Step 2: Read the story and allow time for comments and questions.

Step 3: Identify the story elements and idioms in the story together.

Step 4: Pass out worksheets, pencils, and thesauruses.

Step 5: Explain directions for worksheet.

Step 6: Allow time to complete worksheets.

Step 7: Share worksheets.

Teacher's Notes:

Write the story elements on
the barrels.

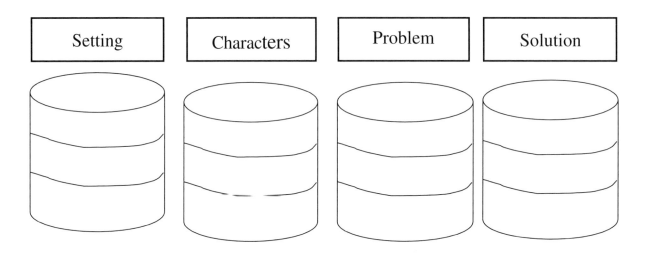

| Setting | Characters | Problem | Solution |

Find the idioms in the dictionary or on the Internet and write the meaning.

Dictionary of Idioms

1. Save for a rainy day _____

2. Scarce as a jackalope or scarce as hen's teeth _____

_____

Dictionary

3. Pack rat _____

4. Hightail _____

Internet

5. Dry wash _____
   www.dictionary.com

Petite Rouge: A Cajun Red Riding Hood

by Mike Artell

Artell, Mike. *Petite Rouge: A Cajun Red Riding Hood*. New York: Dial Books for Young Readers, 2001.

Objective: Students will compare and contrast this version with the original version of "Little Red Riding Hood." They will identify the story elements for the story by completing the worksheet.

Language Arts National Standards

NL-ENG.K-12.3 Evaluation Strategies

Students apply a wide range of strategies to comprehend, interpret, evaluate, and appreciate texts. They draw on their prior experience, their interactions with other readers and writers, their knowledge of word meaning and of other texts, their word identification strategies, and their understanding of textual features (e.g., sound-letter correspondence, sentence structure, context, graphics).

NL-ENG.K-12.9 Multicultural Understanding

Students develop an understanding of and respect for diversity in language use, patterns, and dialects across cultures, ethic groups, geographic regions, and social roles.

NL-ENG.K-12.11 Participating in Society

Students participate as knowledgeable, reflective, creative, and critical members of a variety of literacy communities.

Skills

- Story elements
- Text-to-text story comparison.

Grade Level: Fourth grade

Materials

- Worksheet for each student
- Canoe overhead
- Large basket in which to hide the book, covered with a blue checked cloth

Step 1: Ask students if they remember a story where a little girl carries a basket of goodies. Lead the students in a discussion of "Little Red Riding Hood." Briefly sharing the events of the original version will give the students a frame of reference for comparison later in the lesson.

Step 2: Uncover the book and introduce the title and explain that this is a Cajun version. Explain that the language and characters reflect the lifestyle and culture of Louisiana. Ask them to notice the characters and how they fit into the story's plot.

Step 3: Read the story and share the pictures.

Step 4: Give time for student responses. Lead the group in a brief discussion of the things they notice that reflect the Cajun culture. Refer to the glossary of terms at the beginning of the story if necessary. Some words will be easy for students to figure out as you read, and others will need to be covered in this discussion time.

Step 5: Using the overhead, compare and contrast the original version with this Cajun Red Riding Hood. Fill in the canoe with the elements that are different.

Closure: Independent practice—hand out the worksheet, go over the directions, and allow time for students to complete work. Return to the group and correct the worksheets.

Teacher's Notes:

Fill in the first column in each row first and then complete the second and third columns.

Main Character	Description	Actions
Supporting Characters	Description	Actions
Setting	Where/When	Description
Problem	Begins when	Ends when
Solution	Who helped	How

Petite Rouge rode in a pirogue (flat canoe) to visit her grandmother. Compare Petite Rouge with the Little Red Riding Hood in the original version and put the answers on the correct sides of the canoe.

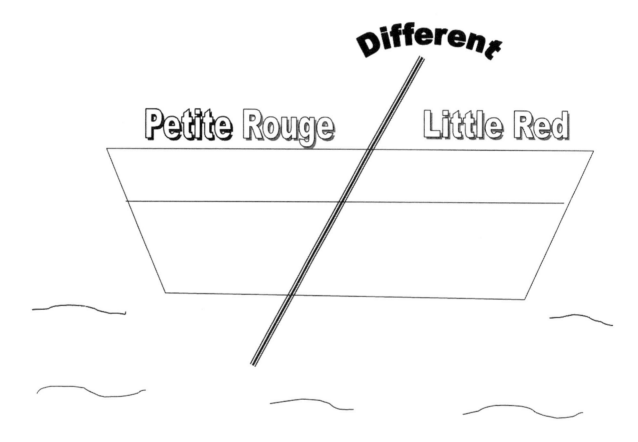

The Seven Chinese Sisters

by Kathy Tucker

Tucker, Kathy. *The Seven Chinese Sisters.* Morton Grove, IL: Albert Whitman, 2003.

Objective: Students will recognize the supporting characters and the effects they have on the plot of the story.

Language Arts National Standards

NL-ENG.K-12.1 Reading for Perspective

Students read a wide range of print and nonprint texts to build an understanding of texts, of themselves, and of the cultures of the United States and the world; to acquire new information; to respond to the needs and demands of society and the workplace; and for personal fulfillment. Among these texts are fiction and nonfiction, classic and contemporary works.

NL-ENG.K-12.3 Evaluation Strategies

Students apply a wide range of strategies to comprehend, interpret, evaluate, and appreciate texts. They draw on their prior experience, their interactions with other readers and writers, their knowledge of word meaning and of other texts, their word identification strategies, and their understanding of textual features (e.g., sound-letter correspondence, sentence structure, context, graphics).

NL-ENG.K-12.9 Multicultural Understanding

Students develop an understanding of and respect for diversity in language use, patterns, and dialects across cultures, ethic groups, geographic regions, and social roles.

Skills

- Story elements (main character and supporting characters)

Grade Level: Fourth grade

Materials

- Worksheet for each student
- Scrap paper and pencils

Step 1: Introduce the story by asking the students to write down the thing they do best. Explain that in today's story, each sister has a talent that she is especially good at doing. Listen for how the seven sisters and their talents rescue baby Seventh Sister from the dragon. Have students take notes as you read.

Step 2: Read the story and share the pictures.

Step 3: Give out the worksheet and go over the directions.

Step 4: Students work with a partner to complete the worksheet. Rotate around the room and help where needed. Students will likely find it difficult to remember all seven sisters. Taking notes while you read will help ensure their success.

Closure: Go over the worksheet together and use this as a means to review the main elements of the story.

Reading Resource Books

Compestine, Ying Chang. *The Runaway Rice Cake.* New York: Simon & Schuster for Young Readers, 2001.

Czemecki, Stefan. *The Cricket's Cage: A Chinese Folktale.* New York: Hyperion Books for Young Children, 1997.

Lee, Milly. *Nim and the War Effort.* New York: Farrar, Straus & Giroux, 1997.

Young, Ed. *Lon Po Po: A Red-Riding Hood Story from China.* New York: Philomel Books, 1989.

Teacher's Notes:

Fill in the blocks with the correct information.

Setting	Location	Evidence
Setting		
First Sister	Talent	How did she use the talent?
Second Sister	Talent	How did she use the talent?
Third Sister	Talent	How did she use the talent?
Fourth Sister	Talent	How did she use the talent?
Fifth Sister	Talent	How did she use the talent?
Sixth Sister	Talent	How did she use the talent?
Seventh Sister	What was different about this sister?	What did she grow up to be at the end of the story?

From *Using Picture Books to Teach Language Arts Standards in Grades 3–5*, written and illustrated by Brenda S. Copeland and Patricia A. Messner. Westport, CT: Libraries Unlimited. Copyright © 2006.

Rumpelstiltskin's Daughter

by Diane Stanley

Stanley, Diane. *Rumpelstiltskin's Daughter.* New York: Morrow Junior Books, 1997.

Objective: Students will predict the outcome of the story and complete the worksheet about story elements.

Language Arts National Standards

NL-ENG.K-12.1 Reading for Perspective

Students read a wide range of print and nonprint texts to build an understanding of texts, of themselves, and of the cultures of the United States and the world; to acquire new information; to respond to the needs and demands of society and the workplace; and for personal fulfillment. Among these texts are fiction and nonfiction, classic and contemporary works.

NL-ENG.K-12.3 Evaluation Strategies

Students apply a wide range of strategies to comprehend, interpret, evaluate, and appreciate texts. They draw on their prior experience, their interactions with other readers and writers, their knowledge of word meaning and of other texts, their word identification strategies, and their understanding of textual features (e.g., sound-letter correspondence, sentence structure, context, graphics).

Skills

- Story elements
- Story prediction

Grade Level: Fourth grade

Materials

- Worksheet for each group

Step 1: Pull one or more versions of the original story and review the basic story of Rumpelstiltskin. Share the title and author of the new story and spend a few minutes writing out on the board predictions of what could happen in this story about the daughter. (Review what "sequel" means in the world of books.)

Step 2: Read the story and share the pictures.

Step 3: Review the predictions and circle the ones that were correct.

Step 4: Hand out the worksheet and go over the directions. Give time for independent work.

Closure: Students should check their work with a partner. Go over as a class as time permits.

Reading Resource Books

Galdone, Paul. *Rumpelstiltskin.* New York: Clarion Books, 1985.

Hamilton, Virginia. *The Girl Who Spun Gold.* New York: Blue Sky Press, 2000.

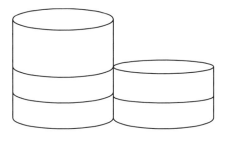

Fill in the information below

Setting	Main Character
Evidence	Supporting Character
Problem	Solution

Explain why Hope was a good name for the main character.

_____

_____

_____

_____

_____

_____

The Magic Nesting Doll

by Jacqueline K. Ogburn

Ogburn, Jacqueline K. *The Magic Nesting Doll*. New York: Puffin Books, 2000.

Objective: Students will recognize the supporting characters and the effects they have on the plot of the story.

Language Arts National Standards

NL-ENG.K-12.1 Reading for Perspective

Students read a wide range of print and nonprint texts to build an understanding of texts, of themselves, and of the cultures of the United States and the world; to acquire new information; to respond to the needs and demands of society and the workplace; and for personal fulfillment. Among these texts are fiction and nonfiction, classic and contemporary works.

NL-ENG.K-12.3 Evaluation Strategies

Students apply a wide range of strategies to comprehend, interpret, evaluate, and appreciate texts. They draw on their prior experience, their interactions with other readers and writers, their knowledge of word meaning and of other texts, their word identification strategies, and their understanding of textual features (e.g., sound-letter correspondence, sentence structure, context, graphics).

Skills

- Supporting characters
- Story elements

Grade Level: Fifth grade

Materials

- Worksheet for each student
- Set of nesting dolls, if possible

Step 1: Introduce the story and, Russia, the country from which it originates. Share your nesting dolls if they are available. (See the author's note in the front of *The Magic Nesting Doll*. This note explains the nesting dolls, what they are called, and how they are made.)

Step 2: Read the story and share the pictures.

Step 3: Pass out the worksheets and go over the directions. Using the story of "The Three Little Pigs" as an example, talk about the wolf's description and effect on the plot. Give students time to complete the worksheet and then use it as a discussion about how the supporting characters help the plot of the story.

Reading Resource Books

Kimmel, Eric A. *Baba Yaga: A Russian Folktale.* New York: Holiday House, 1991.

Mayer, Marianna. *Baba Yaga and Vasilisa the Brave.* New York: Morrow Junior Books, 1994.

Weninger, Brigitte. *The Elf's Hat.* New York: North-South Books, 2000.

Winthrop, Elizabeth. *The Little Humpbacked Horse.* New York: Clarion Books, 1997.

Teacher's Notes:

Worksheet

Several supporting characters in this story help to strengthen the plot. Look at the supporting characters on the left-hand side of the worksheet. Describe what the character looks like and then explain the effect that each has on the plot of the story and its development.

	Describe	**Effect**
Nesting Doll		
Bear		
Wolf		
Firebird		
Grand Vizier		

Souperchicken

by Mary Jane Auch and Herm Auch

Auch, Mary Jane, and Herm Auch. *Souperchicken*. New York: Holiday House, 2003.

Objective: Students will identify the story elements.

Language Arts National Standards

NL-ENG.K-12.3 Evaluation Strategies

Students apply a wide range of strategies to comprehend, interpret, evaluate, and appreciate texts. They draw on their prior experience, their interactions with other readers and writers, their knowledge of word meaning and of other texts, their word identification strategies, and their understanding of textual features (e.g., sound-letter correspondence, sentence structure, context, graphics).

NL-ENG.K-12.6 Applying Knowledge

Students apply knowledge of language structure, language conventions (e.g., spelling and punctuation), media techniques, figurative language, and genre to create, critique, and discuss print and nonprint texts.

NL-ENG.K-12.11 Participating in Society

Students participate as knowledgeable, reflective, creative, and critical members of a variety of literacy communities.

Skills

- Story elements
- Parody

Grade Level: Fifth grade

Materials

- Dictionary with the word "parody" marked so it can be readily located
- Piece of 8 x 10 paper with the word "parody" written on it
- Chicken Soup overhead
- Scrap paper and pencils
- Empty chicken soup cans

Step 1: Set out the empty soup cans before starting to read the story. Hand out scrap paper and ask the students to make a quick list of all of the chicken dishes that they can remember. Allow a couple of minutes for this exercise. Call on several students to share what they have written down.

Step 2: Introduce the book by sharing the title and authors. Explain to the students that this husband and wife author team are noted for their poultry-parody picture books. Ask a student to read the definition of a parody to the class. Talk about how the authors lets the chickens take on human characteristics.

Step 3: As you read the story, ask students to listen for words and phrases that are used throughout the story that help turn sense into nonsense. Example from the book: "noodle away your time."

Step 4: After reading the story, use the soup overhead to record what the students have observed.

Step 5: Book talk other titles by Mary Jane Auch.

Reading Resource Books

Auch, Mary Jane. *Bantam of the Opera*. New York: Holiday House, 1997.

Auch, Mary Jane. *Hen Lake*. New York: Holiday House, 1995.

Auch, Mary Jane. *The Nutquacker*. New York. Holiday House, 1999.

Auch, Mary Jane. *Peeping Beauty*. New York: Holiday House, 1993.

Teacher's Notes:

Chicken Soup

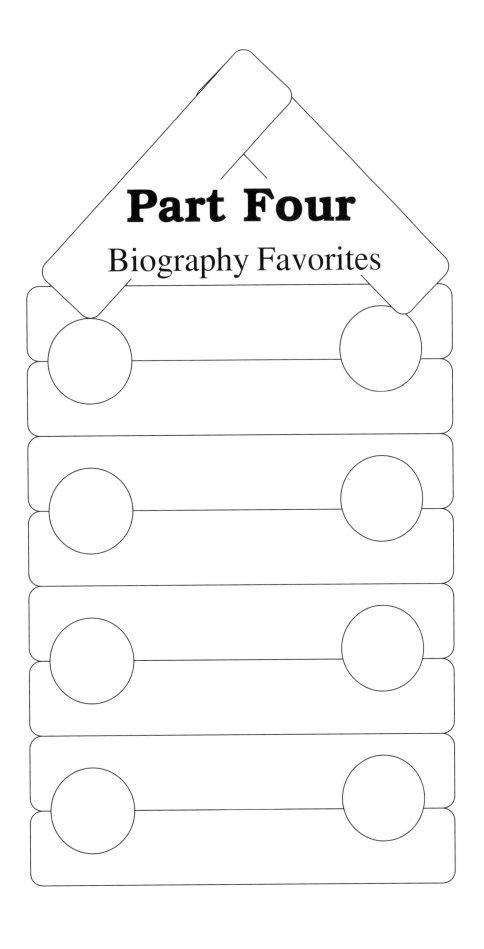

Part Four

Biography Favorites

Abe Lincoln Remembers

by Ann Warren Turner

Turner, Ann Warren. *Abe Lincoln Remembers*. New York: HarperCollins, 2001.

Objective: Students will listen to a biography about Abraham Lincoln and sequence the main events in the book.

Language Arts National Standards

NL-ENG.K-12.2 Understanding the Human Experience

Students read a wide range of literature from many periods in many genres to build an understanding of the many dimensions (e.g., philosophical, ethical, aesthetic) of human experience.

NL-ENG.K-12.3 Evaluation Strategies

Students apply a wide range of strategies to comprehend, interpret, evaluate, and appreciate texts. They draw on their prior experience, their interactions with other readers and writers, their knowledge of word meaning and of other texts, their word identification strategies, and their understanding of textual features (e.g., sound-letter correspondence, sentence structure, context graphics).

Skills

- Sequencing the plot

Grade Level: Third grade

Materials

- Worksheet for each student
- Pencils
- Enlarge worksheet for easel or make an overhead transparency of the worksheet
- Black top hat from a costume store
- Piece of paper with "The Play" typed on it and folded like a program
- Old book
- Lincoln Logs
- Small U.S. flag
- Ring
- Diploma (white paper rolled with red ribbon tied around it)
- Picture of White House and Capitol building

Preparing Materials: Place play program, book, Lincoln Logs, flag, ring, diploma, and pictures in the top hat.

Step 1: Introduce the title, author, and illustrator.

Step 2: Tell students to listen for important events as you read the book.

Step 3: Read the book.

Step 4: Discuss story and illustrations. Students will want to comment about the death of Abraham Lincoln. Tell students that this particular biography does not have the death of Lincoln. Tell them the illustrations were painted and that there were no color cameras at this time in history.

Step 5: Pass out worksheets and pencils.

Step 6: Pull items from hat and talk about the importance of the items to the book. Explain the directions and model the first main event in Abraham Lincoln's life. (Example: Abe lived in a log cabin.) Record the first main event on the enlarged worksheet or overhead.

Step 7: Leave items out so students can refer to them and allow students time to complete the worksheet.

Step 8: Gather students together and share their completed worksheets.

Teacher's Notes:

Write the main events in Abraham Lincoln's life on the logs.

1

2

3

4

Brave Harriet

by Marissa Moss

Moss, Marissa. *Brave Harriet.* San Diego, CA: Silver Whistle, 2001.

Lesson 1

Objective: Students will listen to a biography of Harriet Quimby. Students will discuss story, illustrations, and author's notes at the end of the book.

Language Arts National Standards

NL-ENG.K-12.2 Understanding the Human Experience

Students read a wide range of literature from many periods in many genres to build an understanding of the many dimensions (e.g., philosophical, ethical, aesthetic) of human experience.

NL-ENG.K-12.3 Evaluation Strategies

Students apply a wide range of strategies to comprehend, interpret, evaluate, and appreciate texts. They draw on their prior experience, their interactions with other readers and writers, their knowledge of word meaning and of other texts, their word identification strategies, and their understanding of textual features (e.g., sound-letter correspondence, sentence structure, context graphics).

Skills

- Listening
- Discussing

Grade Level: Third grade

Materials

- World atlas with a map of England and France

Step 1: Introduce the title, author, illustrator, and call number. Talk about the biography section. What are biographies, and where are they located in the library/media center?

Step 2: Read the book.

Step 3: Discuss the book and illustrations. Explain to students that information (true or nonfiction) books may have drawings, not just photographs. Fiction stories can also have either type of illustration.

Step 4: Read author's note in the back of the book.

Step 5: Discuss author's note. Write the dates found in the author's note on the chalkboard.

Step 6: Using math, figure out the flight time for Harriet's famous flight over the English Channel. What time did she leave, and what time did she land?

Step 7: Show Dover, England, and Calais, France, on the map in an atlas. Discuss distance traveled. Compare the distance to a place near the school.

Lesson 2

Objective: Students will review a timeline and make one for the life of Harriet Quimby. Students will research Harriet Quimby on the Internet and record the dates and facts that they find on a timeline.

Language Arts National Standards

NL-ENG.K-12.1 Evaluating Data

Students conduct research on issues and interests by generating ideas and questions, and by posing problems. They gather, evaluate, and synthesize data from a variety of sources (e.g., print and nonprint texts, artifacts, people) to communicate their discoveries in ways that suit their purpose and audience.

Skills

- Researching
- Reviewing timelines

Grade Level: Third grade

Materials

- Pencils
- Scrap paper
- Timeline pattern enlarged or copies made for each student
- Easel

Step 1: Review the concept of a timeline with students. Show an example of a timeline. This could be a timeline of the teacher's life or of a famous person with whom the students are familiar.

Step 2: Show dates and facts from Lesson 1.

Step 3: Explain to the students that they are going to research Harriet Quimby on the Internet and complete a timeline of her life.

Step 4: Divide students between computers depending on the number of computers in your library/ media center or computer lab.

Step 5: Project the following Web site on the wall or screen: www.michiganaviation.org/ enshrinees/quimby.html.

Step 6: Students visit the Web site looking for dates and facts about Harriet Quimby.

Step 7: Allow time for students to gather facts and dates on their scrap paper.

Step 8: Gather students around the easel. Students will add dates and facts to timeline.

Optional activity: Copy a timeline for each student and complete the timeline together using the facts from the Internet.

Lesson 3

Objective: Students will make paper airplanes and fly them across a pretend English Channel.

Language Arts National Standards

NL-ENG.K-12.3 Evaluation Strategies

Students apply a wide range of strategies to comprehend, interpret, evaluate, and appreciate texts. They draw on their prior experience, their interactions with other readers and writers, their knowledge of word meaning and of other texts, their word identification strategies, and their understanding of textual features (e.g., sound-letter correspondence, sentence structure, context graphics).

Skills

- Reading
- Following directions
- Paper folding

Grade Level: Third grade

Materials

- Paper airplane directions
- Plain white paper (8 1/2 x 11)
- Large piece of blue paper for the English Channel
- Prizes or rewards: bookmarks, pencils, more paper airplanes

Web Sites

www.bestpaperairplanes.com

www.paperplane.org

Preparing Materials: Copy directions for a paper airplane from the Web sites. Copy directions for each student.

Step 1: Help students use the directions to fold paper airplanes.

Step 2: Students color their paper airplanes.

Step 3: Students may practice flying their planes in a designated safe place.

Step 4: Students take turns flying their planes across the English Channel.

Step 5: As students complete their flight, leave airplanes on the floor for markers in the distance contest.

Step 6: Award students with prizes for farthest flown, best paint job, smoothest landing, and so on.

Hank Aaron: Brave in Every Way

by Peter Golenbock

Golenbock, Peter. *Hank Aaron: Brave in Every Way*. San Diego, CA: Gulliver Books, Harcourt, 2001.

Objective: Students will listen to a biography about Hank Aaron then recall and write the beginning, middle, end, and supporting details of the story.

Language Arts National Standards

NL-ENG.K-12.2 Understanding the Human Experience

Students read a wide range of literature from many periods in many genres to build an understanding of the many dimensions (e.g., philosophical, ethical, aesthetic) of human experience.

NL-ENG.K-12.3 Evaluation Strategies

Students apply a wide range of strategies to comprehend, interpret, evaluate, and appreciate texts. They draw on their prior experience, their interactions with other readers and writers, their knowledge of word meaning and of other texts, their word identification strategies, and their understanding of textual features (e.g., sound-letter correspondence, sentence structure, context graphics).

Skills

- Beginning, middle, and end of a story
- Supporting details of a story

Grade Level: Third grade

Materials

- Worksheet copied for each student
- Pencils
- Enlarge worksheet for an easel or make an overhead transparency

Step 1: Introduce the title, author, and illustrator. Discuss students' experiences with baseball and softball. Tell students to listen for the beginning, middle, end, and supporting details as the story is read.

Step 2: Read story.

Step 3: Allow students time to comment on story.

Step 4: Pass out worksheets and pencils.

Step 5: Write the author and title on home plate. Write the beginning on first base together as a class. Example: Hank Aaron was born in 1934.

Step 6: Allow time for students to complete worksheet.

Step 7: Share completed worksheets.

Optional Activity: Reread story and make a timeline of Hank Aaron's life. See patterns for timeline and baseballs for dates and facts.

Reading Resource Books

Burleigh, Robert. *Home Run: The Story of Babe Ruth.* New York: Harcourt Brace, 1998.

Curtis, Gavin. *The Bat Boy & His Violin.* New York: Scholastic, 1998.

Golenbock, Peter. *Teammates.* San Diego, CA: Gulliver/Harcourt, 2001.

Teacher's Notes:

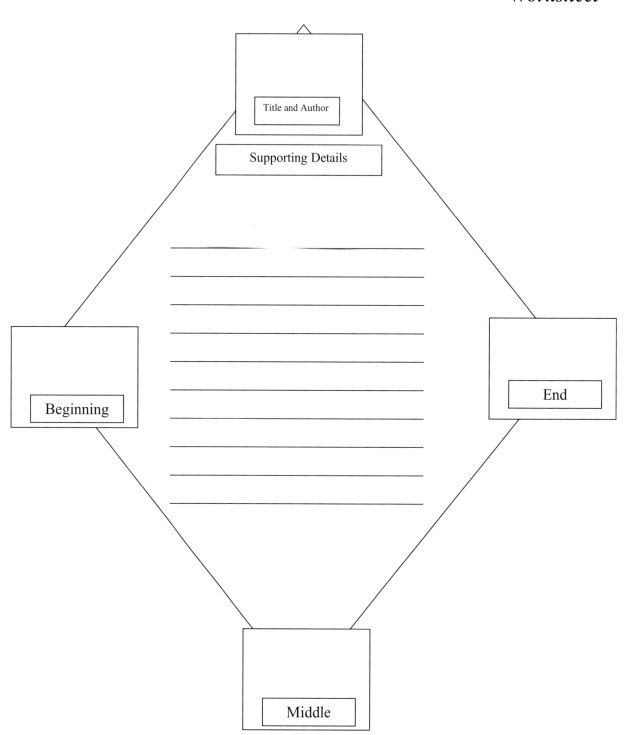

Title and Author

Supporting Details

Beginning

End

Middle

Timeline Pattern

1934 - -1935- -1936

Timeline example

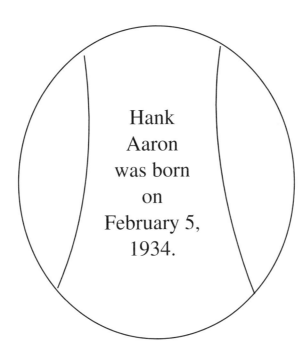

Hank
Aaron
was born
on
February 5,
1934.

Martin's Big Words

by Doreen Rappaport

Rappaport, Doreen. *Martin's Big Words: The Life of Dr. Martin Luther King, Jr.* New York: Hyperion Books, 2001.

Objective: Students will listen to the story and write their own big words.

Language Arts National Standards

NL-ENG.K-12.1 Reading for Perspective

Students read a wide range of print and nonprint texts to build an understanding of texts, of themselves, and of the cultures of the United States and the world; to acquire new information; to respond to the needs and demands of society and the workplace; and for personal fulfillment. Among these texts are fiction and nonfiction, classic and contemporary works.

NL-ENG.K-12.5 Communication Strategies

Students employ a wide range of strategies as they write and use different writing process elements appropriately to communicate with different audiences for a variety of purposes.

NL-ENG.K-12.12 Applying Language Skills

Students use spoken, written, and visual language to accomplish their own purposes (e.g., for learning, enjoyment, persuasion, and the exchange of information).

Skills

- Character study
- Creative writing

Grade Level: Third grade

Materials

- Overhead and a worksheet for each student
- Scrap paper and pencil

Step 1: Introduce this story by using the author's and illustrator's notes at the beginning of the book. Point out the awards that this book has received (Caldecott Honor Book, Coretta Scott King Award, and New York Times Book Review Award).

Step 2: Ask the students to listen for the important words in the story that Dr. King stressed and jot them down on the scrap paper (example: freedom).

Step 3: Read the story and share the pictures with the class.

Step 4: Use the overhead of the stained glass window to record the words that the students picked out from the text.

Step 5: Hand out the worksheet. Brainstorm words that you can add to the ones that Dr. King used. Have the students write them on the left-hand side of the worksheet along with the ones that are already on the page.

Step 6: Stress that Dr. King wanted all people to remember not to fight with fists but to use words to make their point. Students should write their own "Big Words" in the box. Model one on the board. Example: Reading makes you grow tall. Books are special friends to enjoy.

Closure: Share the words the students have written.

Reading Resource Books

Adler, David. *A Picture Book of Martin Luther King, Jr.* New York: Holiday House, 1989.

Farris, Christine King. *My Brother Martin: A Sister Remembers Growing Up with The Rev. Dr. Martin Luther King, Jr.* New York: Simon & Schuster Books for Young Readers, 2003.

Marzollo, Jean. *Happy Birthday, Martin Luther King.* New York: Scholastic, 1993.

Parks, Rosa. *I Am Rosa Parks.* New York: Dial Books for Young Readers, 1997.

Teacher's Notes:

Martin's Big Words

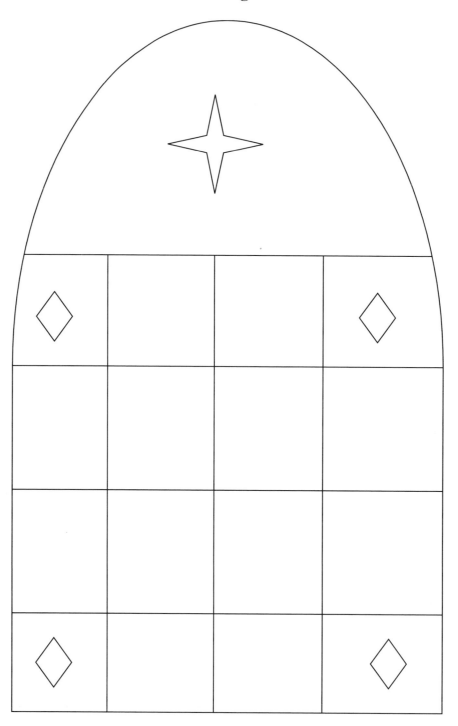

Martin's Big Words

Martin Luther King, Jr. wanted to say "Big Words" when he grew up. Add some other special words that you feel would be important to the world on the left-hand side of the page. Think about these words and then write your own "Big Words" in the box.

Peace

Courage

Dream

My Big Words

Name:

Abbie Against the Storm

by Marcia K. Vaughan

Vaughan, Marcia K. *Abbie Against the Storm*. Hillsboro, OR: Beyond Words, 1999.

Objective: Students will list the main events in the story and then write a summary.

Language Arts National Standards

NL-ENG.K-12.2 Understanding the Human Experience

Students read a wide range of literature from many periods in many genres to build an understanding of many dimensions (e.g., philosophical, ethical, aesthetic) of human experience.

NL-ENG.K-12.3 Evaluation Strategies

Students apply a wide range of strategies to comprehend, interpret, evaluate, and appreciate texts. They draw on their prior experience, their interactions with other readers and writers, their knowledge of word meaning and of other texts, their word identification strategies, and their understanding of textual features (e.g., sound-letter correspondence, sentence structure, context, graphics).

NL-ENG.K-12.4 Communication Skills

Students adjust their use of spoken, written, and visual language (e.g., conventions, style, vocabulary) to communicate effectively with a variety of audiences and for different purposes.

Skills

- Summary writing
- Story elements

Grade Level: Fourth grade

Materials

- An example of a summary from a common picture book or biography.

Step 1: Pass out the lighthouse worksheet and introduce the heroine of this story.

Step 2: As you read, ask students to listen for the main character and setting of the story. They should leave the summary writing until after they have heard the story.

Step 3: Read the story and share the pictures.

Step 4: Lead the students in a discussion of the setting and main character. The setting for this story is more than just the lighthouse. Where is the lighthouse located?

Step 5: Allow a few minutes for students to list the main events of the story on the back of the worksheet. Model the first event of the story. Example: Abbie learns to take care of the lights.

Step 6: Read the example of a summary.

Step 7: Make a list of the main events on the board using student responses. Guide the students into deciding which of the listed items are important to the story. Erase those that are not primary elements. Use the remaining items to create the summary. Write it on the board as students talk through the process. Stress the following: A summary should be brief, concise, and contain some of the facts.

Closure: Allow students time to record the class summary onto their worksheets.

Reading Resource Books

Hesse, Karen. *A Light in the Storm: The Civil War Diary of Amelia Martin.* New York: Scholastic, 1999.

Roop, Peter, and Connie Roop. *Keep the Lights Burning, Abbie.* Minneapolis, MN: Carolrhoda Books, 1985.

Teacher's Notes:

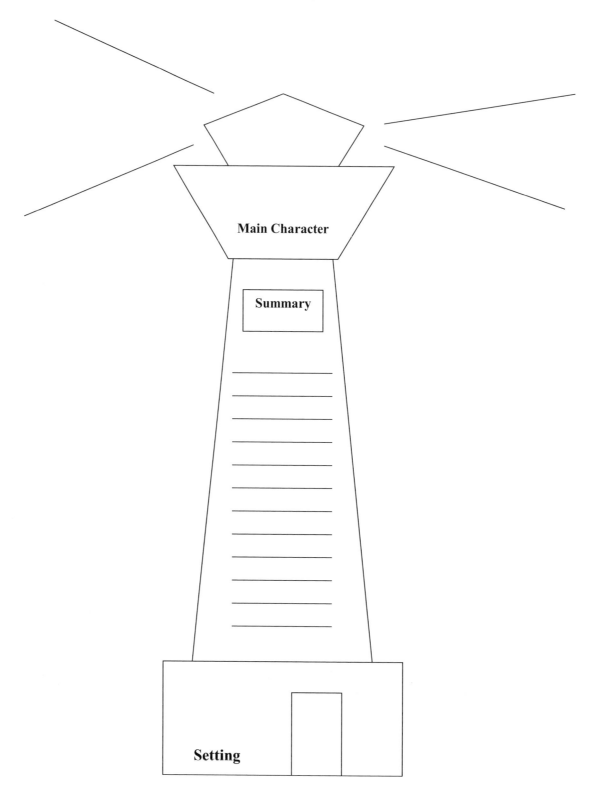

Main Character

Summary

Setting

The Heroine of the Titanic

by Joan W. Blos

Blos, Joan W. *The Heroine of the Titanic*. New York: Morrow Junior Books, 1991.

Objective: Students will listen to a biography about Molly Brown and make a timeline of her life.

Language Arts National Standards

NL-ENG.K-12.2 Understanding the Human Experience

Students read a wide range of literature from many periods in many genres to build an understanding of the many dimensions (e.g., philosophical, ethical, aesthetic) of human experience.

NL-ENG.K-12.3 Evaluation Strategies

Students apply a wide range of strategies to comprehend, interpret, evaluate, and appreciate texts. They draw on their prior experience, their interactions with other readers and writers, their knowledge of word meaning and of other texts, their word identification strategies, and their understanding of textual features (e.g., sound-letter correspondence, sentence structure, context graphics).

Skills

- Timeline

Grade Level: Fourth grade

Materials

- Pencils
- Worksheet copied for each student

Step 1: Pass out worksheets and pencils. Introduce the title and author. Tell students to listen for dates and facts about Molly Brown. Students can use the back of their worksheet to record dates and facts.

Step 2: Read and discuss the story.

Step 3: Explain worksheet. Allow time for students to complete worksheet.

Step 4: Share completed timelines.

Optional Activity: If students are interested in the *Titanic*, research the timeline of the sinking of the *Titanic* from the additional reading resources. In the book *Ghost Liners,* there is a timeline of the sinking. Students may add those dates and times to the boat on the timeline worksheet.

127

Reading Resource Books

Ballard, Robert D. *Ghost Liners.* Boston: Little, Brown & Company, 1998.

Brewster, Hugh, and Laurie Coulter. *882½ Amazing Answers to Your Questions about the Titanic.* New York: Scholastic, 1998.

Osborne, Will. *Titanic.* New York: Random House, 2002.

Shapiro, Marc. *Total Titanic.* New York: Byron Press Mutimedia, 1998.

Spedden, Daisy Corning Stone. *Polar, the Titanic Bear.* New York: Little, Brown and Company. 1994.

Teacher's Notes:

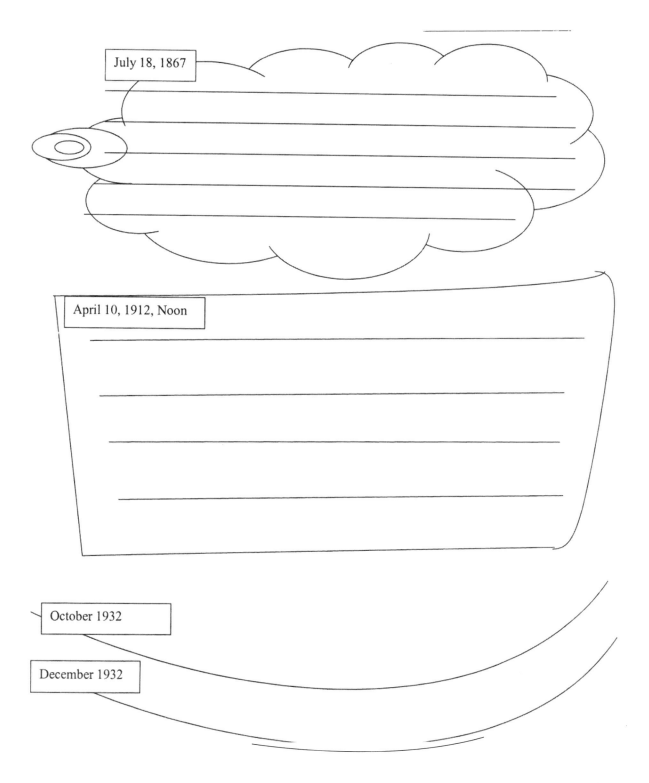

July 18, 1867

April 10, 1912, Noon

October 1932

December 1932

From *Using Picture Books to Teach Language Arts Standards in Grades 3–5*, written and illustrated by Brenda S. Copeland and Patricia A. Messner. Westport, CT: Libraries Unlimited. Copyright © 2006.

My Great-Aunt Arizona

by Gloria Houston

Houston, Gloria. *My Great-Aunt Arizona*. New York: HarperCollins, 1992.

Objective: Students will write a paragraph that compares and contrasts life in the 1880s with life now using the life of Arizona Houston Hughes as a model.

Language Arts National Standards

NL-ENG.K-12.2 Understanding the Human Experience

Students read a wide range of literature from many periods in many genres to build an understanding of many dimensions (e.g., philosophical, ethical, aesthetic) of human experience.

NL-ENG.K-12.3 Evaluation Strategies

Students apply a wide range of strategies to comprehend, interpret, evaluate, and appreciate texts. They draw on their prior experience, their interactions with other readers and writers, their knowledge of word meaning and of other texts, their word identification strategies, and their understanding of textual features (e.g., sound-letter correspondence, sentence structure, context, graphics).

NL-ENG.K-12.4 Communication Skills

Students adjust their use of spoken, written, and visual language (e.g., conventions, style, vocabulary) to communicate effectively with a variety of audiences and for different purposes.

Skills

- Comparing and contrasting
- Writing a paragraph

Grade Level: Fourth grade

Materials

- School-related items (e.g., old books, school bell, slate)
- Collection of books about the turn of the century (see book list for ideas)
- Straw hat or bonnet

Preparing Materials: Place the props around the room and put on the hat.

Step 1: Introduce the story and author of *My Great-Aunt Arizona*. The author has written about her great aunt. Ask students to listen for ways that life was different in the late 1800s compared with life now.

Step 2: Read the story and share the pictures.

Step 3: Hand out worksheets and go over the directions. Allow time for students to complete them on their own. Those who finish ahead of others may read another of the selected books.

Closure: Share paragraphs and point out ones that contained strong opening and closing sentences.

Reading Resource Books

Avi. *The Secret School*. San Diego, CA: Harcourt, 2001.

Bunting, Eve. *Train to Somewhere*. New York: Clarion Books. 1996.

Otto, Carolyn. *Pioneer Church*. New York: Henry Holt, 1999.

Ward, S. *Meet Laura Ingalls Wilder*. New York: Rosen, 2000.

Williams, David. *Grandma Essie's Covered Wagon*. New York: Alferd A. Knopf, 1993.

Teacher's Notes:

My Great-Aunt Arizona

Compare life in the late 1800s with what you do now at school and play.

1. Write what Arizona did on the walls of the school and put what you do on the outside of the building.

2. After you have recorded the differences, write a paragraph on the back of this worksheet that compares life in the 1880s with your life now.

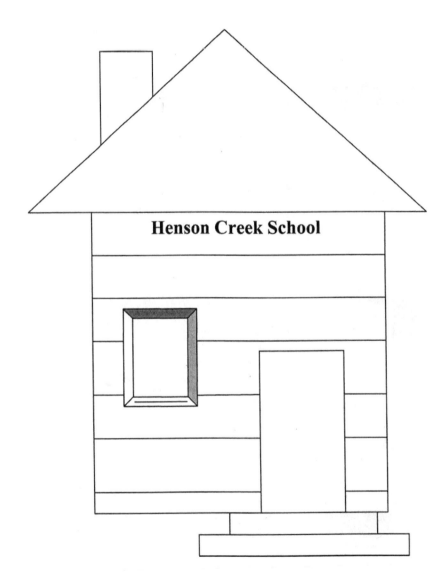

Henson Creek School

From *Using Picture Books to Teach Language Arts Standards in Grades 3–5*, written and illustrated by Brenda S. Copeland and Patricia A. Messner. Westport, CT: Libraries Unlimited. Copyright © 2006.

Thomas Jefferson:
A Picture Book Biography

by James Cross Giblin

Giblin, James Cross. *Thomas Jefferson: A Picture Book Biography.* New York: Scholastic, 1994.

Objective: Students will listen to a biography about Thomas Jefferson and make a timeline of his life. Students will research contemporaries of Jefferson and make an integrated timeline of their lives.

Language Arts National Standards

NL-ENG.K-12.2 Understanding the Human Experience

Students read a wide range of literature from many periods in many genres to build an understanding of the many dimensions (e.g., philosophical, ethical, aesthetic) of human experience.

NL-ENG.K-12.3 Evaluation Strategies

Students apply a wide range of strategies to comprehend, interpret, evaluate, and appreciate texts. They draw on their prior experience, their interactions with other readers and writers, their knowledge of word meaning and of other texts, their word identification strategies, and their understanding of textual features (e.g., sound-letter correspondence, sentence structure, context graphics).

NL-ENG.K-12.7 Evaluating Data

Students conduct research on issues of interest by generating ideas and questions and by posing problems. They gather, evaluate, and synthesize data from a variety of sources (e.g., print and nonprint texts, artifacts, people) to communicate their discoveries in ways that suit their purpose and audience.

Skills

- Researching
- Timelines

Grade Level: Fourth grade

Materials

- A collection of easy biographies of Thomas Jefferson's contemporaries
- Worksheets copied for each group
- Pencils

- Computers logged onto the Internet
- Encyclopedias

Step 1: Introduce the title, author, and illustrator.

Step 2: Tell students to listen for dates and facts related to Thomas Jefferson as the book is read.

Step 3: Read and discuss book.

Step 4: Make a timeline of Thomas Jefferson's life together using a dry-erase board or chalkboard. Students and teacher may share the task of recording the data.

Step 5: Divide the class into three groups. Give each group a copy of the timeline. Each will be assigned a contemporary of Thomas Jefferson (examples: Ben Franklin, George Washington, John Hancock, James Madison, and John Adams). Tell students they will research their person in a biography, an encyclopedia, or on the Internet and then make a timeline. Students will record the name of the person on the first line at the top of the scroll on the worksheet.

Step 6: Allow time for students to complete the timeline using the biographies, encyclopedias, and computers.

Step 7: Share timelines and make an integrated timeline of Jefferson and his contemporaries.

Teacher's Notes:

Thomas Jefferson
By James Cross Giblin

Worksheet

From *Using Picture Books to Teach Language Arts Standards in Grades 3–5*, written and illustrated by Brenda S. Copeland and Patricia A. Messner. Westport, CT: Libraries Unlimited. Copyright © 2006.

Betty Doll

by Patricia Polacco

Polacco, Patricia. *Betty Doll*. New York: Philomel Books, 2001.

Objective: Students will listen to the story and answer the comprehension questions on the worksheet.

Language Arts National Standards

NL-ENG.K-12.2 Understanding the Human Experience

Students read a wide range of literature from many periods in many genres to build an understanding of many dimensions (e.g., philosophical, ethical, aesthetic) of human experience.

NL-ENG.K-12.3 Evaluation Strategies

Students apply a wide range of strategies to comprehend, interpret, evaluate, and appreciate texts. They draw on their prior experience, their interactions with other readers and writers, their knowledge of word meaning and of other texts, their word identification strategies, and their understanding of textual features (e.g., sound-letter correspondence, sentence structure, context, graphics).

Skills

- Comprehension

Grade Level: Fifth grade

Materials

- Handmade doll

- Cover a box with brown paper so that the lid is able to open and the doll can be placed inside. On the outside of the box write, "For My Dearest Little Trisha." Wrap an old letter or something to represent the letter in the story around the doll.

Step 1: Introduce the story by showing the box and pretending that you are the author and are receiving the doll and letter for the first time. (See author's note at the beginning of the book for details.) Act this out before reading the story.

Step 2: Read the book and share the pictures. Pass out the worksheets and go over the directions. Model by writing the first event of the story on the board. (Example: Mary Ellen makes the doll after the fire.) Students should complete the other events. Give time for independent work.

Step 3: Go over the events of the story and give students the opportunity to share answers. Write the events on the board.

Closure: Ask students to turn the worksheet over and write a sentence about something that has a place of honor in their family (example: a family quilt or a pocket watch). Share comments on the thing if possible.

Reading Resource Books

Polacco, Patricia. *Babushka's Doll*. New York: Simon & Schuster for Young Readers, 1990.

Polacco, Patricia. *My Ol' Man*. New York: Philomel Books, 1995.

Polacco, Patricia. *Thank You, Mr. Falker*. New York: Philomel Books, 1998.

Teacher's Notes:

Betty Doll
By Patricia Polacco

Worksheet

1. Who created Betty Doll? _____

   Why? _____

2. List some unhappy events that Betty Doll helped Mary Ellen overcome.

   _____

   _____

   _____

   _____

3. When did Patricia receive the doll?

   _____

4. Explain how Betty Doll helped Patricia.

   _____

5. Summarize this story. _____

   _____

   _____

   _____

6.   In this story Patricia shared what she learned about overcoming grief. Her mother's love brought comfort and warmth. Can you compare this story to something in your life? Explain your thoughts in the space below.

   _____

   _____

   _____

From *Using Picture Books to Teach Language Arts Standards in Grades 3–5*, written and illustrated by Brenda S. Copeland and Patricia A. Messner. Westport, CT: Libraries Unlimited. Copyright © 2006.

Hiding from the Nazis

by David A. Adler

Adler, David. *Hiding from the Nazis*. New York: Holiday House, 1997.

Lesson 1

Objective: Students will listen to the story and complete an acrostic about the main character.

Language Arts National Standards

NL-ENG.K-12.1 Reading for Perspective

Students read a wide range of print and nonprint texts to build an understanding of texts, of themselves, and of the cultures of the United States and the world; to acquire new information; to respond to the needs and demands of society and the workplace; and for personal fulfillment. Among these texts are fiction and nonfiction, classic and contemporary works.

NL-ENG.K-12.5 Communication Strategies

Students employ a wide range of strategies as they write and use different writing process elements appropriately to communicate with different audiences for a variety of purposes.

NL-ENG.K-12.12 Applying Language Skills

Students use spoken, written, and visual language to accomplish their own purposes (e.g., for learning, enjoyment, persuasion, and the exchange of information).

Skills

- Character study

- Writing an acrostic

Grade Level: Fifth grade

Materials

- Scrap paper and pencils

- A six-pointed star cut from yellow felt (write Jew across the front of it with a black marker)

Step 1: Attach the yellow star on your outfit before the story starts. Introduce the story, pointing out that if you were the main character in this story you would have had to sew a yellow star on all of your clothing before you were seen in public. That would show the world that you were different and should be avoided or shunned.

Step 2: Hand out scrap paper and ask students to list adjectives that would describe the main character as you read the book aloud.

Step 3: Read the story and discuss what they wrote down. Make a master list on the board.

Step 4: Using the overhead acrostic sheet, ask the students to help you fill in words and phrases that would describe the character. Model one so that the students get the idea of how an acrostic works.

Lesson 2: Acrostic Writing

Follow-up activity for another class period

Objective: Students will write an acrostic using facts from an easy biography.

Language Arts National Standards

NL-ENG.K-12.1 Reading for Perspective

Students read a wide range of print and non print texts to build an understanding of texts, of themselves, and of the cultures of the United States and the world; to acquire new information; to respond to the needs and demands of society and the workplace; and for personal fulfillment. Among these texts are fiction and nonfiction, classic and contemporary works.

NL-ENG.K-12.5 Communication Strategies

Students employ a wide range of strategies as they write and use different writing process elements appropriately to communicate with different audiences for a variety of purposes.

Skills

- Writing an acrostic

Grade Level: Fifth grade

Materials

- Collection of easy picture book biographies, such as

  - *Abbie Against the Storm* by Marcia K. Vaughan
  - *Snowflake Bentley* by Jacqueline Briggs Martin
  - *Boss of the Plains* by Laurie Carlson
  - *Helen Keller* by David A. Adler
  - *Paul Revere and the Bell Ringers* by Jonah Winter
  - *Florence Nightingale* by Rebecca Vickers

- Paper and pencils

Step 1: Review both the story *Hiding from the Nazis* and the acrostic that the class made in the first lesson. Hand out the easy biographies and divide up the class into small groups. Explain that the group needs to read the book and make a list of adjectives. The acrostic will introduce the main character to the rest of the class and excite students to read about this special person.

Step 2: Allow time for group work. Rotate around the room and offer help where needed.

Closure: Let the students create a display with the completed acrostics and books.

Reading Resource Books

Adler, David A. *A Hero and the Holocaust*. New York: Holiday House, 2002.

Adler, David A. *A Picture Book of Anne Frank*. New York: Holiday House, 1993.

Adler, David A. *One Yellow Daffodil*. New York: Gulliver Books, 1995.

Jules, Jacqueline. *The Grey Striped Shirt*. Los Angeles, CA: Alef Design Group, 1993.

Teacher's Notes:

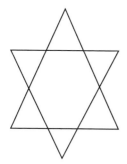

Lore Baer

L

O

R

E

B

A

E

R

Appendix

NL-ENG.K-12.1 Reading for Perspective

Bigfoot Cinderrrrrella
Brave Harriet
Gullywasher Gulch
Hiding from the Nazis
The Magic Nesting Doll
Martin's Big Words
Muncha! Muncha! Muncha!
Rumpelstiltskin's Daughter
The Seven Chinese Sisters
Sody Sallyratus
Tacky and the Emperor
Testing Miss Malarkey

NL-ENG.K-12.2 Understanding the Human Experience

Abbie Against the Storm
Abe Lincoln Remembers
Betty Doll
Brave Harriet
Hank Aaron: Brave in Every Way
The Heroine of the Titanic
Look Out, Jack! The Giant Is Back!
My Great-Aunt Arizona
The Rag Coat
Shoeless Joe & Black Betty
Sister Anne's Hands
Sody Sallyratus
Testing Miss Malarkey
Thomas Jefferson: A Picture Book Biography

NL-ENG.K-12.3 Evaluation Strategies

Abbie Against the Storm
Abe Lincoln Remembers
Aunt Flossie's Hats and Crab Cakes Later
Betty Doll
Bigfoot Cinderrrrrella
The Blizzard
Brave Harriet
The Christmas Miracle of Jonathan Toomey
Gullywasher Gulch
Hank Aaron: Brave in Every Way

The Heroine of the Titanic
The Lady in the Box
Look Out, Jack! The Giant Is Back!
The Magic Nesting Doll
Muncha! Muncha! Muncha!
My Great-Aunt Arizona
Petite Rouge: A Cajun Red Riding Hood
Pink and Say
The Purple Coat
The Rag Coat
Rumpelstiltskin's Daughter
The Seven Chinese Sisters
The Seven Silly Eaters
Shoeless Joe & Black Betty
Sister Anne's Hands
Sody Sallyratus
Souperchicken
Tacky and the Emperor
Thomas Jefferson: A Picture Book Biography

NL-ENG.K-12.4 Communication Skills

Abbie Against the Storm
Bad Boys
The Blizzard
Chocolatina
The Memory String
More Than Anything Else
My Great-Aunt Arizona
Pink and Say
The Remarkable Farkle McBride
Silver Packages
When Jessie Came Across the Sea

NL-ENG.K-12.5 Communication Strategies

Bad Boys
Chocolatina
Hiding from the Nazis
Martin's Big Words
The Memory String
More Than Anything Else
The Remarkable Farkle McBride
Silver Packages
When Jessie Came Across the Sea

NL-ENG.K-12.6 Applying Knowledge

Souperchicken

NL-ENG.K-12.7 Evaluating Data

Pink and Say
Thomas Jefferson: A Picture Book Biography

NL-ENG.K-12.8 Developing Research Skills

The Blizzard
The Bunyans
The Christmas Miracle of Jonathan Toomey
Pink and Say
When Jessie Came Across the Sea

NL-ENG.K-12.9 Multicultural Understanding

Gullywasher Gulch
Petite Rouge: A Cajun Red Riding Hood
The Seven Chinese Sisters
Sody Sallyratus

NL-ENG.K-12.11 Participating in Society

The Christmas Miracle of Jonathan Toomey
Petite Rouge: A Cajun Red Riding Hood
Souperchicken

NL-ENG.K-12.12 Applying Language Skills

Aunt Flossie's Hats and Crab Cakes Later
The Blizzard
Hiding from the Nazis
The Lady in the Box
Martin's Big Words
Pink and Say
The Purple Coat
The Seven Silly Eaters

Bibliography

Aaseng, Nathan. *Sports Great Kirby Puckett*. Berkeley Heights, NJ: Enslow, 1993.

Adler, David A. *A Hero and the Holocaust*. New York: Holiday House, 2002.

Adler, David. *Hiding from the Nazis*. New York: Holiday House, 1997.

Adler, David A. *Lou Gehrig: The Luckiest Man*. New York: Harcourt, 1997.

Adler, David A. *One Yellow Daffodil*. New York: Gulliver Books, 1995.

Adler, David A. *A Picture Book of Anne Frank*. New York: Holiday House, 1993.

Adler, David. *A Picture Book of Martin Luther King, Jr.* New York: Holiday House, 1989.

Artell, Mike. *Petite Rouge: A Cajun Red Riding Hood*. New York: Dial Books for Young Readers, 2001.

Auch, Mary Jane. *Bantam of the Opera*. New York: Holiday House, 1997.

Auch, Mary Jane. *Hen Lake*. New York: Holiday House, 1995.

Auch, Mary Jane. *The Nutquacker*. New York. Holiday House, 1999.

Auch, Mary Jane. *Peeping Beauty*. New York: Holiday House, 1993.

Auch, Mary Jane, and Herm Auch. *Souperchicken*. New York: Holiday House, 2003.

Avi. *The Secret School*. San Diego, CA: Harcourt, 2001.

Ballard, Robert D. *Ghost Liners*. Boston: Little, Brown & Company, 1998.

Bildner, Phil. *Shoeless Joe & Black Betty*. New York: Simon & Schuster for Young Readers, 2002.

Birdseye, Tom. *Look Out, Jack! The Giant Is Back!*. New York: Holiday House, 2001.

Bloom, Benjamin. *Taxonomy of Educational Objectives: Handbook 1, The Cognitive Domain*. New York: David McKay, 1956.

Blos, Joan W. *The Heroine of the Titanic*. New York: Morrow Junior Books, 1991.

Bogart, Jo Ellen. *Jeremiah Learns to Read*. New York: Orchard Books, 1997.

Bradby, Marie. *More Than Anything Else*. New York: Orchard Books, 1995.

Breitenbucher, Cathy. *Bonnie Blair*. Minneapolis, MN: Lerner, 1994.

Brewer, Paul. *The American Civil War*. Austin, TX: Raintree/Steck-Vaughn, 1999.

Brewster, Hugh, and Laurie Coulter. *882½ Amazing Answers to Your Questions About the Titanic*. New York: Scholastic, 1998.

Bunting, Eve. *The Blue and the Gray*. New York: Scholastic, 1996.

Bunting, Eve. *Dreaming of America: An Ellis Island Story*. New York: Bridge Water Books, 2000.

Bunting, Eve. *The Memory String.* New York: Clarion Books, 2000.

Bunting, Eve. *Train to Somewhere.* New York: Clarion Books. 1996.

Burleigh, Robert. *Home Run: The Story of Babe Ruth.* New York: Harcourt Brace, 1998.

Climo, Shirley. *The Egyptian Cinderella.* New York: Harper Trophy, 1989.

Climo, Shirley. *The Persian Cinderella.* New York: HarperCollins, 1999.

Cobb, Mary. *The Quilt-Block History of Pioneer Days: With Projects Kids Can Make.* Brookfield, CT: Millbrook Press, 1995.

Compestine, Ying Chang. *The Runaway Rice Cake.* New York: Simon & Schuster for Young Readers, 2001.

Curtis, Gavin. *The Bat Boy & His Violin.* New York: Scholastic, 1998.

Czemecki, Stefan. *The Cricket's Cage: A Chinese Folktale.* New York: Hyperion Books for Young Children, 1997.

DeClements, Barthe. *6th Grade Can Really Kill You.* New York: Viking Kestrel, 1985.

Erdosh, George. *Food and Recipes of the Civil War.* New York: PowerKids Press, 1997.

Erlbach, Arlene. *Blizzards.* Chicago: Children's Press, 1995.

Ernst, Lisa Campbell. *Little Red Riding Hood: A Newfangled Prairie Tale.* New York: Simon & Schuster Books for Young Readers, 1995.

Farris, Christine King. *My Brother Martin: A Sister Remembers Growing Up with The Rev. Dr. Martin Luther King, Jr.* New York: Simon & Schuster Books for Young Readers, 2003.

Finchler, Judy. *Miss Malarkey's Field Trip.* New York: Walker, 2004.

Finchler, Judy. *Miss Malarkey Won't Be In Today.* New York: Walker, 1998.

Finchler, Judy. *Testing Miss Malarkey.* New York: Walker, 2000.

Finchler, Judy. *You're a Sport, Miss Malarkey.* New York: Walker, 1998.

Fleming, Candace. *Muncha! Muncha! Muncha!* New York: Atheneum Books for Young Readers, 2002.

Galdone, Paul. *Rumpelstiltskin.* New York: Clarion Books, 1985.

Giblin, James Cross. *Thomas Jefferson: A Picture Book Biography.* New York: Scholastic, 1994.

Giff, Patricia Reilly. *The Beast in Ms. Rooney's Room.* New York: Dell, 1984.

Golenbock, Peter. *Hank Aaron Brave in Every Way.* San Diego, CA: Gulliver/Harcourt, 2001.

Golenbock, Peter. *Teammates.* New York: Scholastic, 1990.

Gregson, Susan R. *Phillis Wheatley.* Mankato, MN: Bridgestone Books, 2002.

Hamilton, Virginia. *The Girl Who Spun Gold.* New York: Blue Sky Press, 2000.

Harris, Jim. *Jack and the Giant: A Story Full of Beans*. Flagstaff, AZ: Rising Moon, 1997.

Haslam, Andrew, and Barbara Taylor. *Weather*. Chicago: World Book, 1997.

Hesse, Karen. *A Light in the Storm: The Civil War Diary of Amelia Martin*. New York: Scholastic, 1999.

Hest, Amy. *The Purple Coat*. New York: Four Winds Press, 1986.

Hest, Amy. *When Jessie Came Across the Sea*. Cambridge, MA: Candlewick Press, 1997.

Hickox, Rebecca. *The Golden Sandal: A Middle Eastern Cinderella*. New York: Holiday House, 1998.

Hill, Kirkpatrick. *The Year of Miss Agnes*. New York: Margaret K. McElderry, 2000.

Hiser, Berniece T. *The Adventure of Charlie and His Wheat-Straw Hat: A Memorat*. New York: Dodd, Mead, 1986.

Hite, Sid. *The Journal of Rufus Rowe: A Witness to the Battle of Fredericksburg*. New York: Scholastic, 2003.

Hoberman, Mary Ann. *The Seven Silly Eaters*. New York: Browndeer Press, 1997.

Houston, Gloria. *My Great-Aunt Arizona*. New York: HarperCollins, 1992.

Houston, Gloria. *The Year of the Perfect Christmas Tree: An Appalachian Story*. New York: Dial Books for Young Readers, 1988.

Howard, Elizabeth Fitzgerald. *Aunt Flossie's Hats and Crab Cakes Later*. New York: Clarion Books, 2001.

Isaacs, Anne. *Swamp Angel*. New York: Dutton Children's Books, 1994.

Jackson, Ellen B. *Cinder Edna*. New York: Lothrop, Lee & Shepard, 1994.

Jacobs, William Jay. *Ellis Island: New Hope in a New Land*. New York: Scribner's, 1990.

Johnston, Tony. *Bigfoot Cinderrrrella*. New York: Putnam, 1998.

Jules, Jacqueline. *The Grey Striped Shirt*. Los Angeles, CA: Alef Design Group, 1993.

Kellogg, Steven. *Jack and the Beanstalk*. New York: Morrow Junior Books, 1991.

Kimmel, Eric A. *Baba Yaga: A Russian Folktale*. New York: Holiday House, 1991.

Kraft, Erik. *Chocolatina*. New York: Scholastic, 2004.

Lasky, Kathryn. *Christmas After All: The Great Depression Diary of Minnie Swift*. New York: Scholastic, 2001.

Laverde, Arlene. *Alaska's Three Pigs*. Seattle, WA: PAWS IV/Sasquatch Books, 2000.

Lee, Milly *Nim and the War Effort*. New York: Farrar, Straus & Giroux, 1997.

Leighton, Maxinne Rhea. *An Ellis Island Christmas*. New York: Viking, 1992.

Lester, Helen. *Tacky and the Emperor*. Boston: Houghton Mifflin, 2000.

Levine, Ellen. *If Your Name Was Changed at Ellis Island*. New York: Scholastic, 1993.

Lithgow, John. *The Remarkable Farkle McBride*. New York: Simon & Schuster Books for Young, 2000.

Lorbiecki, Marybeth. *Sister Anne's Hands*. New York: Dial Books for Young Readers, 1998.

Louie, Ai-Ling. *Yeh-Shen: A Cinderella Story from China*. New York: Philomel, 1982.

Lowell, Susan. *Cindy Ellen: A Wild Western Cinderella*. New York: HarperCollins, 2000.

Martin, Rafe. *The Rough-face Girl*. New York: G.P. Putnam's Sons, 1992.

Mayer, Marianna. *Baba Yaga and Vasilisa the Brave*. New York: Morrow Junior Books, 1994.

Marzollo, Jean. *Happy Birthday, Martin Luther King*. New York: Scholastic, 1993.

McGovern, Ann. *The Lady in the Box*. New York: Turtle Books, 1997.

Mills, Lauren. *The Rag Coat*. New York: Little, Brown & Company, 1991.

Mitchell, Marianne. *Gullywasher Gulch*. Honesdale, PA: Boyds Mills Press, 2002.

Moss, Marissa. *Brave Harriet*. San Diego, CA: Silver Whistle, 2001.

Nolen, Jerdine. *Thunder Rose*. Orlando, FL: Silver Whistle/Harcourt, 2003.

Ogburn, Jacqueline K. *The Magic Nesting Doll*. New York: Puffin Books, 2000.

Osborne, Mary Pope. *Kate and the Beanstalk*. New York: Atheneum Books for Young Readers, 2000.

Osborne, Will. *Titanic*. New York: Random House, 2002.

Otto, Carolyn. *Pioneer Church*. New York: Henry Holt, 1999.

Palatini, Margie. *Bad Boys*. New York: HarperCollins, 2003.

Parks, Rosa. *I Am Rosa Parks*. New York: Dial Books for Young Readers, 1997.

Polacco, Patricia. *Babushka's Doll*. New York: Simon & Schuster for Young Readers. 1990.

Polacco, Patricia. *Betty Doll*. New York: Philomel Books, 2001.

Polacco, Patricia. *The Keeping Quilt*. New York: Simon & Schuster Books for Young Readers, 1988.

Polacco, Patricia. *My Ol' Man*. New York: Philomel Books, 1995.

Polacco, Patricia. *Pink and Say*. New York: Philomel Books, 1994.

Polacco, Patricia. *Thank You, Mr. Falker*. New York: Philomel Books, 1998.

Rappaport, Doreen. *Martin's Big Words: The Life of Dr. Martin Luther King, Jr.* New York: Hyperion Books, 2001.

Roop, Peter, and Connie Roop. *Keep the Lights Burning, Abbie*. Minneapolis, MN: Carolrhoda Books, 1985.

Rylant. Cynthia. *Silver Packages: An Appalachian Christmas Story*. New York: Orchard Books, 1997.

Schroeder, Alan. *Smoky Mountain Rose: An Appalachian Cinderella*. New York: Dial Books for Young Readers, 1997.

Selden, Bernice. *The Story of Annie Sullivan: Hellen Keller's Teacher*. Milwaukee, WI: Gareth Stevens, 1997.

Shapiro, Marc. *Total Titanic*. New York: Byron Press Multimedia, 1998.

Simon, Seymour. *Weather*. New York: Morrow Junior Books, 1993.

Sloat, Teri. *Sody Sallyratus*. New York: Dutton Children's Books, 1997.

Smucker, Barbara C. *Selina and the Shoo-fly Pie*. New York: Stoddart Kids, 1999.

Spedden, Daisy Corning Stone. *Polar, The Titanic Bear*. New York: Little, Brown & Company, 1994.

Stanley, Diane. *Rumpelstiltskin's Daughter*. New York: Morrow Junior Books, 1997.

Terabn, Marvin. *Dictionary of Idioms*. New York: Scholastic, 1996.

Trivizas, Eugene. *The Three Little Wolves and the Big Bad Pig*. New York: Margaret K. McElderry Books, 1993.

Tucker, Kathy. *The Seven Chinese Sisters*. Morton Grove, IL: Albert Whitman, 2003.

Turner, Ann Warren. *Abe Lincoln Remembers*. New York: HarperCollins, 2001.

Turner, Ann Warren. *Sewing Quilts*. New York: Macmillan, 1994.

Vaughan, Marcia. *Abbie Against the Storm*. Hillsboro, OR: Beyond Words, 1999.

Vaughan, Marcia K. *The Secret to Freedom*. New York: Lee & Low Books, 2001.

Wachet, Roger. *The Medal of Honor*. New York: Children's Press, 2002.

Ward, S. *Meet Laura Ingalls Wilder*. New York: Rosen, 2000.

Webster's Dictionary and Thesaurus. Scotland: Geddes & Grosset, 2002.

Weninger, Brigitte. *The Elf's Hat*. New York: North-South Books, 2000.

Wiesner, David. *The Three Pigs*. New York: Clarion Books, 2001.

Williams, David. *Grandma Essie's Covered Wagon*. New York: Alfred A. Knopf, 1993.

Williams, Suzanne. *Library Lil*. New York: Dial Books for Young Readers, 1997.

Winthrop, Elizabeth. *The Little Humpbacked Horse*. New York: Clarion Books, 1997.

Wittman, Sally. *The Wonderful Mrs. Trumbly*. New York: Harper & Row, 1982.

Wojciechowski, Susan. *The Christmas Miracle of Jonathan Toomey*. Cambridge, MA: Candlewick Press, 1995.

Wood, Audrey. *The Bunyans*. New York: Blue Sky Press, 1996.

Woodruff, Elvira. *The Memory Coat*. New York: Scholastic, 1999.

The World Book Encyclopedia. Chicago: World Book.

Wright, Betty Ren. *The Blizzard*. New York: Holiday House, 2003.

Young, Ed. *Lon Po Po: A Red-Riding Hood Story from China.* New York: Philomel Books, 1989.

Web Resources

Bryce Canyon: http://www.desertusa.com/bryce/

Congressional Medal of Honor: www.cmohs.org

Ellis Island: www.ellisisland.com

Great Sand Dunes: http://www.npca.org/explore_the_parks/new_parks/greatsanddunes.asp

Mammoth Cave: http://www.mammoth.cave.national-park.com/info.htm#mc

National Council of Teachers of English: www.ncte.org

Niagara Falls: http://www.niagarafallslive.com/Facts_about_Niagara_Falls.htm

Old Faithful: http://www.nps.gov/yell/tours/oldfaithful/

Paper Airplanes: www.bestpaperairplanes.com

Paper Airplanes: www.paperplane.com

Rocky Mountains: http://biology.usgs.gov/s+t/SNT/noframe/wm146.htm

Susan Wojciechowski: http://goose.ycp.edu/~swojciecl

USA Today: http://www.usatoday.com/weather

Index

Aaron, Hank, 116–19
Aaseng, Nathan, 59
Abbie Against the Storm, 124–26, 140
Abe Lincoln Remembers, 109–11
Adler, David, 59, 121, 139–42
Alaska's Three Pigs, 13
American Civil War, The, 64
Applying knowledge (standard), xi, 103
Applying language skills (standard), xi, xii, 37, 43, 46, 51, 61, 63, 120, 139
Artell, Mike, 91–93
Atlases, 17, 23–24, 112
Auch, Herm, 103–5
Auch, Mary Jane, 103–5
Aunt Flossie's Hats and Crab Cakes Later, 37
Avi, 131

Baba Yaga and Vasilisa the Brave, 101
Baba Yaga: A Russian Folktale, 101
Babushka's Doll, 137
Bad Boys, 12
Bantam of the Opera, 104
Baseball, 58–60, 116–19
Bat Boy & His Violin, The, 117
Beast in Ms. Rooney's Room, The, 19
Beginning, middle, and end of story (skills), 116
Benjamin Bloom's Taxonomy of Educational Objectives: Handbook 1, The Cognitive Domain, ix
Betty Doll, 136–38
Bigfoot Cinderrrrella, 82–84
Bildner, Phil, 58
Biographies, ix, 107–40
Birdseye, Tom, 40
Blizzard, The, 46–50
Blizzards, 48
Bloom's Levels of Thinking Taxonomy (comprehension questions labeled with), 38, 41, 47–48, 52, 55, 59, 62, 68, 71
Blos, Joan W., 127–29
Blue and the Gray, The, 64
Bogart, Jo Ellen, 19
Bonnie Blair, 59
Boss of the Plains, 140
Bradby, Marie, 18–20
Brave Harriet, 112–15
Breitenbucher, Cathy, 59

Brewer, Paul, 64
Brown, Molly, 127–29
Bunting, Eve, 5–8, 27, 64, 131
Bunyan, Paul, 15–17
Bunyans, The, 15–17
Burleigh, Robert, 117

Cajun culture, 91–93
Carlson, Laurie, 140
Character study, 120, 139
Chocolatina, 3–4
Christmas After All, 10
Christmas Miracle of Jonathan Toomey, The, 85–87
Cinder Edna, 83
Cinderella stories, 82–84
Cindy Ellen: A Wild Western Cinderella, 83
Civil War, American, 61–66
Climo, Shirley, 83
Cobb, Mary, 68
Communication skills (standard), xi, 3, 5, 9, 12, 18, 21, 46, 61
Communication strategies (standard), xi, 3, 5, 9, 12, 18, 21, 120, 139, 140
Comparing and Contrasting, 130
Compestine, Ying Chang, 96
Comprehension, ix, 21, 35–72, 136
Congressional Medal of Honor, 64
Creative writing, 9, 18, 26, 32, 120
Cricket's Cage, The: A Chinese Folktale, 96
Curtis, Gaven, 117
Czemecki, Stefan, 96

DeClements, Barthe, 19
Developing research skills (standard), xii, 15, 46, 63
Dictionaries, 46, 61, 65, 88, 103
Discussion skills, 112
Dreaming of America: An Ellis Island Story, 27

Egyptian Cinderella, The, 83
Elf's Hat, The, 101
Ellis Island, 27, 28, 31
Ellis Island: New Hope in a New Land, 28
Encyclopedias, 23, 27, 48, 134
Erdosh, George, 64
Erlback, Arlene, 48

Ernst, Lisa Campbell, 13
Evaluating data (standard), xi, 63, 113, 133
Evaluation strategies (standard), xi, 23, 37, 40, 43, 46, 51, 58, 61, 67, 75, 80, 82, 85, 88, 91, 95, 98, 100, 103, 109, 112, 114, 116, 127, 133, 136

Farris, Christine King, 121
Finchler, Judy, 32–33
Fleming, Candace, 75–79
Florence Nightingale, 140
Following directions (skills), 114
Food and Recipes of the Civil War, 64

Galdone, Paul, 98
Giff, Patricia Reilly, 19
Girl Who Spun Gold, The, 98
Golden Sandal, The: A Middle Eastern Cinderella Story, 83
Golenbock, Peter, 116–19
Grandma Essie's Covered Wagon, 131
Gregson, Susan R., 71
Grey Striped Shirt, The, 141
Gullywasher Gulch, 88–90

Hamilton, Virginia, 98
Hank Aaron: Brave in Every Way, 116–19
Happy Birthday, Martin Luther King, 121
Harris, Jim, 41
Haslam, Andrew, 48
Helen Keller, 140
Hen Lake, 104
Hero and the Holocaust, A, 141
Heroine of the Titanic, The, 127–29
Hesse, Karen, 125
Hest, Amy, 26–31, 54–57
Hickox, Rebecca, 83
Hiding from the Nazis, 139–42
Hill, Kirkpatrick, 71
Hite, Sid, 64
Hoberman, Mary Ann, 43–45
Home Run: The Story of Babe Ruth, 117
Houston, Gloria, 10, 130–32
Howard, Elizabeth Fitzgerald, 37
Hughes, Arizona Houston, 130–32

I Am Rosa Parks, 121
Idioms, 88, 90
If Your Name Was Changed at Ellis Island, 28
Immigration, 25–31
International Reading Association, ix, xi–xii
Internet, researching on, 63–64, 133–34

Jack and the Beanstalk, 41
Jack and the Giant: A Story Full of Beans, 41
Jackson, Joe, 58–60
Jacobs, William, 28
Jefferson, Thomas, 133–35
Jeremiah Learns to Read, 19
Johnson, Tony, 82–84
Journal of Rufus Rowe, The, 64
Jules, Jacqueline, 141

Kane's Famous First Facts, 23
Kate and the Beanstalk, 41
Keep the Lights Burning, Abbie, 125
Kellogg, Steven, 41
Kimmel, Eric, 101
Kraft, Erik, 3–4

Lady in the Box, The, 51–53
Lasky, Kathryn, 10
Laverde, Arlene, 13
Lee, Milly, 96
Lester, Helen, 80–81
Library Lil, 19
Light in the Storm, A: The Civil War Diary of Amelia Martin, 125
Lincoln, Abraham, 64, 109–11
Linking Picture Books to Standards, ix
Listening skills, 112
Lithgow, John, 21–23
Little Humpbacked Horse, The, 101
Little Red Riding Hood: A Newfangled Prairie Tale, 13
Lon Po Po: A Red-Riding Hood Story from China, 96
Look Out, Jack! The Giant Is Back!, 40
Loribiecki, Marybeth, 70–72
Lou Gehrig: The Luckiest Man, 59
Louie, Ai-Ling, 83
Lowell, Susan, 83

Magic Nesting Doll, The, 100–102
Maps, 15–17
Martin, Jacqueline Briggs, 140
Martin, Rafe, 83
Martin's Big Words: The Life of Dr. Martin Luther King, Jr., 120–23
Marzollo, Jean, 121
Mayer, Marianna, 101
McGovern, Ann, 51–53
Medal of Honor, The, 64
Meet Laura Ingalls Wilder, 131
Memory Coat, The, 28

Memory String, The, 5–8
Mills, Lauren, 67–69
Miss Malarkey Won't Be in Today, 32
Miss Malarkey's Field Trip, 32
Mitchell, Marianne, 88–90
More Than Anything Else, 18–20
Moss, Marissa, 112–15
Multicultural understanding (standard), xii, 23,
      91, 95
Muncha! Muncha! Muncha!, 75–79
*My Brother Martin: A Sister Remembers
      Growing Up with The Reverend Martin
      Luther King, Jr.,* 121
My Great-Aunt Arizona, 130–32
My Ol' Man, 137

National Council of Teachers of English, ix,
      xi–xii
National Language Arts Standards, ix, xi–xii
Nim and the War Effort, 96
Nutquacker, The, 104

Ogburn, Jacqueline K., 100–102
One Yellow Daffodil, 141
Osborne, Mary Pope, 41
Otto, Carolyn, 131

Palatini, Margie, 12
Paper airplanes, 114
Paper folding, 114
Parks, Rosa, 121
Parody, 103
Participating in society (standard), xii, 91, 103
Paul Revere and the Bell Ringers, 140
Peeping Beauty, 104
Persian Cinderella, The, 83
Petite Rouge: A Cajun Red Riding Hood, 91–94
Phillis Wheatley, 71
Picture Book of Anne Frank, A, 141
Picture Book of Martin Luther King, Jr., A, 121
Pioneer Church, 131
Pioneer life, 67–69, 130–32
Polacco, Patricia, 19, 68, 136–38
Purple Coat, The, 54–57

*Quilt-Block History of Pioneer Days, The: With
      Projects Kids Can Make,* 68
Quilts, 67–69
Quimby, Harriet, 112–15

Rag Coat, The, 67
Rappaport, Doreen, 120–23

Reading for perspective, xi, 23, 75, 80, 82, 85,
      88, 95, 98, 100, 120, 139, 140
Reading skills, 114
Recipes, 43–44
Remarkable Farkle McBride, The, 21–23
Researching, 15, 27, 113, 133
Retelling, 5
Roop, Connie, 125
Roop, Peter, 125
Rough-Face Girl, 83
Rumplestiltskin, 98
Rumplestiltskin's Daughter, 98
Runaway Rice Cake, The, 96
Rylant, Cynthia, 9–11

Schroeder, Alan, 83
Secret to Freedom, The, 68
Secret School, The, 131
Selina and the Shoo-fly Pie, 68
Sequencing the plot, ix, 3–33, 109
Seven Chinese Sisters, The, 95–97
Seven Silly Eaters, The, 43–45
Sewing Quilts, 68
Shoeless Joe & Black Betty, 58–60
Silver Packages, 9–11
Simon, Seymour, 48
Sister Anne's Hands, 70–72
6th Grade Can Really Kill You, 19
Sloat, Teri, 23–25
*Smoky Mountain Rose: An Appalachian
      Cinderella,* 83
Smucker, Barbara C., 68
Snowflake Bentley, 140
Sody Sallyratus, 23–25
Souperchicken, 103–5
Sports Great Kirby Puckett, 59
Standards for the English Language Arts, ix,
      xi–xii
Stanley, Diane, 98
Story of Annie Sullivan, The, 71
Story
      elements, ix, 73–105, 124
      beginning, middle, and ending of, 116
      prediction, 98
      supporting details of, 116
Summary writing, 124
Supporting characters, 100

Tacky and the Emperor, 80–81
Taylor, Barbara, 48
Teammates, 117
Testing Miss Malarkey, 32–33

Text-to-text connections, 12, 82, 91
Thank You, Mr. Falker, 19, 137
Thomas Jefferson: A Picture Book Biography,
　　133–35
Three Pigs, The, 13
Timelines, 113, 119, 127, 133
Titanic (ship), 127–29
Train to Somewhere, 131
Trivizas, Eugene, 13
Tucker, Kathy, 95–97
Turner, Ann Warren, 68, 109–11

Understanding the human experience (standard),
　　xi, 23, 40, 58, 67, 109, 112, 116, 124, 127,
　　133, 136
USATODAY, 48–49

Vaughan, Marcia K., 68, 124–26, 140
Vickers, Rebecca, 140

Wachet, Roger, 64
Ward, S., 131
Washington, Booker T., 18–20
Weather, 46–50
Weather (Haslam and Taylor), 48
Weather (Simon), 48

Web site, navigating, 27, 48–49, 63–64, 85, 87
Weninger, Brigitte, 101
When Jessie Came Across the Sea, 26–31
Wiesner, David, 13
Williams, David, 131
Williams, Suzanne, 19
Winter, Jonah, 140
Winthrop, Elizabeth, 101
Wojciechowski, Susan, 85–87
Wonderful Mrs. Trumbly, The, 71
Wood, Audrey, 15
Woodruff, Elvira, 28
World Book Encyclopedia, 23, 64
Wright, Betty Ren, 46–50
Writing, 54
　　an acrostic, 139, 140
　　creative, 9, 18, 26, 32, 120
　　directions, 43
　　a paragraph, 130
　　a summary, 85

Year of Miss Agnes, The, 71
Year of the Perfect Christmas Tree, The, 10
Yeh-Shen: A Cinderella Story from China, 83
You're a Sport, Miss Malarkey, 32

About the Authors

Brenda S. Copeland has been an elementary librarian for the past eight years in the Palmyra School District, Palmyra, Pennsylvania. She earned her Master's of Library Science degree from Kutztown University and her Bachelor's in Elementary Education at the University of Delaware.

Patricia A. Messner has been an elementary media specialist for the past sixteen years in the Lebanon City School District, Lebanon, Ohio. She earned her Master's of Education degree from Miami University, Oxford, Ohio, and her Bachelor's in Elementary Education at Asbury College, Wilmore, Kentucky.

Brenda and Patricia are sisters and grew up in southwestern Ohio. They have completed this book over the telephone and the Internet. Every Sunday afternoon the world comes to a stand still as Brenda and Patricia talk over the week's events and plan the next step, whether it is a section in their book or a story that needs some sparkle. Ideas and lessons are reworked and added to as the sisters share their library skills. Lesson plans are traded by e-mail and practiced in their library and media center classrooms, both in Ohio and Pennsylvania, several times before they end up on the desk of Sharon Coatney, Libraries Unlimited Editor.

This dynamic pair love to dress alike and appear at conferences and book signings. They dream of one day getting their children's stories published.

Other books written by these authors are *Linking Picture Books to Standards* (Libraries Unlimited, 2003) and *Collaborative Library Lessons for the Primary Grades* (Libraries Unlimited, 2004).